DEATH
AND OTHER BEAUTIFUL THINGS

ALSO BY MOHAMED GHAZI

Honest
Half Pleasure Half Pain
Blue

DEATH

AND OTHER BEAUTIFUL THINGS

MOHAMED GHAZI

Copyright © 2021 by Mohamed Ghazi.

Ghazi, Mohamed.

Death and Other Beautiful Things / Mohamed Ghazi Al-Hussain.

USA: November, 2021.

187 pages.

ISBN-13: 979-8492975401

ISBN-10: 8492975401

Cover Design:
Mohamed Ghazi

Interior Design:
Mohamed Ghazi

Dedicated to
the broken.

I hope this book heals you.

Warning:

This book contains content that might be troubling for some readers, including, but not limited to, references to death, suicide, self-harm, childhood trauma, and PTSD, among other things. Please be mindful of these and other possible triggers. Also, remember to seek professional assistance whenever possible.

They say *the dying* are the only
ones who really know how to
live.

Luke Adams, 26, committed suicide by shooting himself in the head last Friday. Before the bullet touched his head, Adams wrote this book as a suicide note alone in his cold lonely house.

Introduction

Why do people kill themselves?

Before you answer this question and blame it on the lack of religion or manic episodes, do a little research about the main cause of suicide. It is *Depression.*

Severe Depression can cause people to experience intense emotional agony and a loss of hope, leaving them unable to see any other way out of the misery other than taking their own life.

The word "suicide" gives many people the impression that "it was his own decision" or "he chose to die". And because Depression is still such a misunderstood condition, it's difficult to blame people for not fully comprehending it. A simple internet search will reveal how many people have no sympathy for those who commit suicide.

Suicide is a fatal symptom of Depression. Depression is a medical condition, not a choice or a way of life. You can't just "cheer up" when you're depressed, just like you can't choose not to have cancer. When someone commits suicide due to Depression, they die from Depression – an illness that kills millions each year.

It is difficult to know how many people die from Depression each year because the figures and statistics only show how many people die from "suicide" (and you do not have to suffer from Depression to commit suicide; it is typically suggested). Perhaps Depression might lose some of its "it was his own fault" stigma if we start focusing on the illness, rather than the symptom.

I have a voice inside my head called anxiety. I have my own Depression that I'm tired of fighting. I'm here to share my story.

This is my story, and this is how I shot myself.

Part One

DEATH

The Day He Shoots Himself

As you read this, I'm descending to my death. This is not a book; this is my suicide note.

My phone vibrates.

Mom is calling.

I switch off the phone.

It's all her fault, I think. I'm here, writing this, because of her, because she left me. Why did she leave me?

Hello mother, can you help me now? Or is it too late for me to be helped?

I swallow more pills. Nothing seems to be numbing the ache I feel inside my guts. The pills got used to me like an old friend now, what a disgrace I've become. I'm in hate with myself and my body. I'm at my lowest. I don't think I'm human anymore. I descended from being human a long time ago. I'm a monster. I have never been this low.

Or have I?

I used to be a happy kid, you know? I can't recall anything, but I can see the photographs. I take a look behind my desk at the corkboard. I look at my photographs in various stages of my life. I smile as I recall myself as a four-year-old riding a bike. I was a happy child. But I'm no longer a child or happy. I'm blue.

Have you ever read the book "Blue"? What a gloomy, sad book. I'm curious if the author is still alive. Some of us who carry so much pain within us are destined to die.

I believe I deserve to die. At least, that's what my father used to tell me.

"You don't deserve to breathe."

"I hope you kill yourself."

I wish I could tell my father that his wish will finally be granted. But I'm afraid I can't. My father is rotting in hell. Maybe I will see him soon and I get to tell him myself.

"LUKE," I hear my mother calling me. Oh, how I miss hearing her voice. I feel a warm sensation in my stomach. The pills are working. I'm taking off.

I wonder who will find my body. I wonder if anyone will cry. I wonder if they'll mention me in the news. A 26-year-old man diagnosed with clinical Depression was found dead in his apartment after shooting himself in the head.

But there's no need for wondering.
Wondering is for the living,
and I don't believe I am alive anymore.

Hello, who are you?
Why are you here?
Do you know me?
I bet you do.
It doesn't matter.
Welcome.
You are safe with me.
I'll be right here.
I'm well-known, yet not everyone knows who I am. I live within people's heads and feed on them. I'm as infamous as the darkness under your bed. I'm the dark circles under your eyes. I'm your never-ending sleepless nights. I'm the daily reminder of lost lovers. I'm what comes with betrayal and deception. I'm the companion of separation. I'm the lies that have been told in the name of love. I'm what comes with the death of your loved ones. I'm the thoughts you are trying so hard to get rid of. I am your bad eating habits. I'm the one to blame for your loss of appetite. I'm the sound of millions of muffled screams into your pillow. I'm the first cry and the last. I'm your shiver on the warmest day and your sweat on the coldest night.

Have you recognized me?

Hello, It's me.
I'm Depression.
Nice to meet you.
I will help Luke tell his story.

AND I'M ANXIETY.

I'M ANXIETY.

I'M ANXIETY.

The Day He Shoots Himself

When someone commits suicide, the first thing people wonder is how they did it. Then they question why they did it. And those questions are asked out of curiosity. We are all intrigued by other people's tragedies because we want to believe that we are better than them.

By the end of this book, you will know how I will kill myself, and you'll also know why, throughout these words and lines. I don't expect you to care, but I expect you to understand why I'm doing it.

I'm fed up with everything and everyone around me. I'm sick of the unending chronic pain I endure every time I move. I'm sick of this body which is carrying my very heavy soul. I'm sick of my Depression and anxiety.

"Why don't you ask for help?" is probably your next question.

I did. I asked my psychiatrist, and he did nothing. I asked my family, and they told me to be a man. I asked my friends, and they told me to stop the drama. I asked my girlfriends, and they left me. I asked for the help of my colleagues, and they couldn't care less.

No one wants to help anyone. Everyone in this world is completely so self-centered. They care about their own happiness, their own well-being, their own bodies. No one cares about anyone but themselves, and those who care, do care because it fills that empty void of self-satisfaction that will make them feel a little better about themselves to sleep better through the night.

No one cares about anyone.
And you probably don't care about me too.
You are reading my misery
for your muse.

38 Days Before He Shoots Himself

"Mouth"

My mouth is heavy
and it is hard to hold
my head above anymore.

I don't speak;
I grieve.

I don't walk;
I shiver.

My mouth is burdened
by the weight of the words
I should have said
to you.

I grieve.

And just like the
ocean grieves every morning
when the moon
leaves,
I grieve.

Depression

Falling asleep isn't an escape. I'm here and there. I can control your nightmares too, and your dreams. Subconscious and conscious. Awake or asleep. I'm with you.

Way before having those nightmares, Luke was thinking a lot about ending his own life. He can deny it as much as he wants. I know that he has always contemplated what comes after death. He constantly thinks about death's lightness and all the other beautiful things. Poor Luke. He was almost terrified of his thoughts, so he forced himself to think about the good times. You can somehow control your thoughts, but you will never be able to control your dreams and nightmares. So all he could do was daydream about the good old days, out of desperation and yearning.

He was happy once. You were all happy once until something happened to you that changed the course of your life forever.

You were all happy once,
until one day you were not anymore.

Tell me,
were you happy once?

37 Days Before He Shoots Himself

"Happy New Year"

On the first day of the new year
I promised myself
no more toxic relationships
and no more
Depression.

But then I met
you.

The apocalypse started.
The woods were on fire.
And I gave you
a second chance.

And people were dying on the streets.
Corpses piled up like mountains.
And you.

The worst year ever
with the worst company.

And plans washed out in the sink.
And the best thing in life
wasn't allowed.
And I'm not talking
about my pills,
I'm talking about traveling.

Oppression and masks.
And it was the worst year ever.
And you.

36 Days Before He Shoots Himself

"The Nightmare"

"People no longer scare me. They can't hurt me any more than they have already. What scares me the most now is what I am capable of. My thoughts. My nightmares. My anxiety. My Depression," I shiver. "I'm scared of myself."

He pens something in his crimson notebook. He is probably going to write that I'm a lost cause.

"Are you still having the same nightmares?" He asks.

"Yes."

He continues writing.

HE DOESN'T CARE ABOUT YOU. WHAT ARE YOU DOING HERE?

"Do you know what I despise the most about psychiatrists?"

He looks at me disgracefully, half-smiling. "What?" He answers.

"Sometimes, you treat your patients more like test subjects and less like humans."

Silence.

"I apologize if I made you feel this way, Luke." He says with wide eyes.

I stand up abruptly. "No, I apologize if I was disrespectful, Dr. Richard. I'm here because I really want to get better. I can't remember the last time I slept. I'm t..." I stutter. "I'm just tired." I exhale a deep breath that I haven't realized I was holding.

"I'm here to help you get better."

He rises from his brown leather chair, his crimson notebook still on his desk, and he takes a seat next to me.

"Look, Luke. I know you are upset, and you look tired and sleep-deprived. But you shouldn't be upset with me. I'm here to assist you in any way I can." He frowns slightly. I try to relax and sit down again.

"It's the same nightmare I've had before. Every single

night. It's dark in my room and I'm alone. I try to call my mom, but she doesn't hear me. It's almost as though I'm shouting underwater. I'm feeling numb and out of breath. I open the drawer and look at the gun. I'm having an anxiety attack that feels like my heart is trying to escape from my chest. I take the gun and point it toward my head. And then I pull the trigger. And I wake up sweating, terrified of falling asleep again. I'm terrified of facing death one more time." I tremble at the thought of this nightmare.

"Those are dreams, Luke. They have nothing to do with reality. You should focus your energy on real life. Concentrate on the future."

IT'S NOT A DREAM. IT'S REAL. IT'S GOING TO HAPPEN TO YOU.

WHAT IF IT HAPPENS? WHAT WOULD YOU DO, LUKE?

"But it felt real." I say. "I don't think those are just dreams, Dr. Richard."

"What do you mean, Luke?" He asks, worryingly. "Do you think this dream might come true?"

"Maybe," I say,
and I know the answer already.

35 Days Before He Shoots Himself

"The Evil Within"

They say you have flashbacks of your life before you die, especially the best times you've had. And lately, I've been getting a lot of those. It's almost as though my body is preparing me for death.

I don't recall many specifics, but everything comes back to me in varied pictures and noises. Images and sounds that are beautiful and poetic, and full of Harmony.

I was happy. My skin was darker than usual, and my eyes were brighter. She used to call them "oceanic blue". I used to be full of life, and we were on an island. Her cheeks were flushed from the sun, and her hair was wavy and dark like a lovely beautiful black sky. She was wearing a sunflower in her hair. Our days were spent at the beach, and our nights were spent at the club. People were staring at us as if we were the happiest couple in the world. And maybe, just maybe, in few desperate seconds, we were.

I was happy once in an old cabin by the beach, with Harmony by my side. She once lost the door key and then became so enraged and angry that I began videotaping her until we started laughing together. I used to be happy. Her cheeks were flushed from the sun. My eyes were so blue. And she was stunning. And she was beautiful; I bet she still is.

How can someone so beautiful
hold so much evil inside?

I guess I will die with this question
unanswered.

Depression

This is a journey into the depths of darkness. After this one, there will be no more stories. There is only one story. Luke's final story and how he will face death.

What is Luke planning to do? What is he leaving behind? I know what he's thinking. I can hear his thoughts, and I feed off of them.

If you are depressed, welcome. If you aren't, have a look around and you'll see what I mean. I exist within you as well as everywhere else. You can try to ignore or look away from me, but I'm always there, just out of sight, where you're most vulnerable. I'm as real as your other organs. I exist within your thoughts.

Death will always find a way to get to you. Guns and heights. Speed and cuts. You can stand on the edge of the world with the gun aimed at your head, it will be all the same with death. Because you know that death is just around the corner, waiting for you to make that little slip.

All of his sufferings will be for nothing.
It's just a matter of time now.
The clock is ticking and his funeral is coming.
Hasn't he suffered enough?
He has.
Let go of him.
Forget him.

34 Days Before He Shoots Himself

"After Love"

The tragedy of love is
unending.

Many lovers are
buried
under the ground
while they have never
ended up together.

The tragedy of love
knowing that one day
all the kisses will end,
but you will remember
the taste of their lips
forever.

All the words have ended
but the voice echoes
in your hollow heart.

What have you become?
After love.
Before death.

You are just
a walking tragedy.

33 Days Before He Shoots Himself

"The Poem"

Dreams collide with reality. I still can't believe I married her. I sometimes wake up fighting every memory of her. And then I lose to one memory.

There was this time when we're on our honeymoon. We were holding hands walking on the beach while the sun was departing in a beautiful and peaceful scene as the sky collides with the sea, creating vivid colors. The sunset was beautiful, but all I could see was her. Her sun-kissed skin. Her hair was adorned with a golden sunflower. Her favorite color was yellow.

She stopped and was looking at me. And I still remember how I felt every time she looked at me. She used to look through me.

"Tell me something I don't know about you, Luke Adams." She said, holding my hands. I was holding the world.

"What do you want to know, Harmony Deadwood?"

"Do you write about me?" She asked with a coy, beautiful smile, her fingers, softly touching my left cheek.

"I only write about you," I said.

"Read me something."

"I don't need to read it. I memorize all the words I write for you."

She cracked a smile. A wicked but beautiful smile; she was well aware that she owned me physically and my thoughts and memories too. And the poems I wrote for her were not my own. Nothing belonged to me. Everything belonged to her.

"What are you going to give me in return?" I asked, teasing.

She said, "The world". At least, that's what I thought. She gave me the entire world. Then she suffocated me with Depression and insecurities.

> *"Here, with you next to me*
> *we stand under the willow tree*
> *I finally understand the meaning of cohesion.*
> *Like the sky coheres with the sea,*
> *I finally hear your heart beats in my chest*
> *and I finally smell my perfume on your clothes.*
> *We are one,*
> *for I am forever yours*
> *if you would like to be forever mine.*
> *I carry too much love for you,*
> *I think I am more in love*
> *than alive."*

That was the first poem I read to her.

And I'm reading it right now. It sounds familiar, but it's not something I would write. Dreams collide with reality. I can't believe I married her.

I can't believe I used to be happy.

32 Days Before He Shoots Himself

"My Madness and You"

My writings stink
because I still write about you.

One year later and I can still see you
on the walls of my room
and inside my veins.

Blood and war
are all I've known since
the day I met you.

My writings stink.
The ink on my papers still screams your name.
I want to be a successful writer
but how can I be
when I only write about you?

My fingertips stink as I type on my typewriter,
your name
and your memories;
filth on paper.

I want to stop writing but I can't,
because I'm scared
I would lose my madness,
join the normal people,
and have a normal life.

So I write again, filth or not,
I write.

And you are still, always here and there.

31 Days Before He Shoots Himself

"Almost"

I stray,
I stray at the end of the room
far away
but you pull me
back into your dreams
and you sleep
while I'm awake.

One year later,
twelve slow months
and I'm back to the wrong place
with all my love
and you fed me
promises
for breakfast
and kisses
for lunch
and then I fell,
and you left me
on the ground.

Almost,
we were almost.

Then we were
nothing.

The Day He Shoots Himself

I'm not going to shoot myself for anyone's sake. I'm not a fool. I'll do it for myself.

I can't live with all of these thoughts racing through my mind. I'm filled with self-loathe. My Depression is eating me alive. I'm drowning in a sea of darkness, and each time I try to swim, I sink deeper.

You'll probably say, "You didn't fight hard enough, Luke." but I swear, I did. I fought it as hard as I could with all the might I had. I strived to love and to be loved. I tried to forget what had happened in the past. I tried different kinds of pills, cut off the pills, relapsed, went to AA meetings, relapsed again, tried different kinds of medications, and went to many psychiatrists. I tried to live with my Depression, but my Depression doesn't want me to live.

I once tried to beat my Depression, you know? And I almost won. "Almost" is the saddest word in the English language. I almost beat my Depression. And I almost lived.

Things were going against me; I encountered the most despicable people who used and betrayed me. I tried to make friends, but maintaining a healthy friendship is difficult when you have anxiety. I tried and failed at relationships as well. People want someone as simple as a bright day, and I am a storm. I've been turned into a collection of failure stories. I no longer have a place in this world. This world is for the cruel, and I'm soft.

NO ONE LOVES YOU AND NO ONE EVER WILL.
YOU CAN NOT HANDLE ALL OF THIS PAIN.
DO IT.
KILL YOURSELF. DO IT.
DO IT!

31 Days Before He Shoots Himself

"Addiction"

I have tried pills
almost all of them
all the colors and shapes
until I realized
that our
worst addictions
are to the people
we love.

Depression

In this world, he was alone; in the realm of humans. But he wasn't alone in the world inside his head. No, not at all. His thoughts usually accompanied him. And he always wished that things were the other way around. That he will make many friends, many of whom will not abandon him. Friends who won't leave because of his darkness. Everyone, however, was terrified of him, his past, his ideas, and his blue eyes. He has always felt himself to be repulsive. He sometimes felt as if he was a mutant; deformed.

His life is no longer about living. It's more of a state of being. He is worthless. Aged and crumpled like an old, worthless piece of paper. Since Harmony left him, he has lost his Harmony with the rest of the world. One night crept into the next without a pause, he has been left in the dust. He began to feel as though he no longer belonged to the living. And he doesn't. He deserves all of this suffering. He has earned his unhappiness. He is nothing now more than ash and dust.

And soon, soon enough, he'll do what he's always meant to do.

Are you ready for it?
Are you going to do it too?

30 Days Before He Shoots Himself

"Father's Blood"

"You should get out there and meet new people. You can't live your life feeling bitter over Harmony." While I organize the tens of medicines she needs to take today in her pill organizer, my mother says.

I reek of hospitals and medicines. I almost feel like I'm the one who is ill.

YOU ARE GOING TO GET SICK. IS SHE CONTAGIOUS?

YOU ARE TIRED OF THIS. THIS IS TOO MUCH FOR YOU!!

"A failed marriage isn't the end of the world." She continues.

"*Or is it?*" I think. YOU WILL NEVER FIND LOVE AGAIN. YOU ARE A LOSER. YOU ARE NOTHING.

"Luke, my dear, I'm talking to you," she says, frustrated that I'm not answering her. "I won't be here for long, and we both know it."

I slam her pill organizer against the table. "Please, Mother, don't say that." I burst with anger. And I immediately regret it. "We will find a donor soon. Everything will be alright."

Silence dominates the room, and the air begins to feel heavier. I'm having another anxiety attack that I'm doing everything I can to suppress. IF YOU DON'T FIND A DONOR, SHE WILL DIE. YOU HAVE TO FIND SOMEONE NOW. WHAT ARE YOU DOING? DO SOMETHING. YOU ARE USELESS.

Both of my mother's kidneys have failed. We now spend more time in hospitals than we do at home. Honestly, I've given up on finding a kidney donor. We have been struggling for six months now, it feels impossible to hold on to hope. If I could, I would have given her all of my organs, but I'm not a match. My father's blood runs through my veins. I'm full of my father's filth. Another thing that makes me even more resentful of myself.

29 Days Before He Shoots Himself

"Death is Certain"

I smoke
until my lungs give up.

This cigarette is for
you
the thing it does to
my lungs
similar to what you did to
my heart.

Love is
temporary
but the pain
isn't.

So I smoke
and swallow more pills,
maybe I will live,
after you,
but death is certain,
my dear.

The Day He Shoots Himself

I keep asking myself, "why me?". And if you've ever dealt with Depression, you'll understand what I mean.

I like to go out by myself and observe people from a distance. I study them. I try to put myself in their shoes. I try to understand them. I try to understand myself.

I ran into a group of macho men the other day who reeked of toxic masculinity. They were frequently drinking, smoking, flirting, and even bullying others. And it is always the bully who becomes the prom king, the CEO or the president. And it is always the bullied who end up with Depression. I stayed and watched them try to be whoever they were trying to be. And I hated them. I hated how happy and confident they were. I hated my Depression even more, and how my life turned out.

I'm this damaged man who is neither alive enough to live nor dead enough to be buried.

I've discovered that some people live their lives by disconnecting their hearts from their brains. No overthinking, no feelings flooding their body every second. No anxiety. No worrying. They just live.

But *why me?* Why do I have to go through all this pain? Why am I so fragile? Why is my mental health always in jeopardy? Why am I so sensitive? Why do I break easily?

And the most important question that keeps me awake every night is
when will it all be over?

28 Days Before He Shoots Himself

"Nine-Year-Old"

I couldn't sleep again, anxiety attacks amidst my sleep. Reality collides with illusions, they become one; a painful endeavor.

I had another dream about that night. And I awoke drenched in sweat and tears. I don't remember much about it, but I remember how I felt. Broken, alone, nauseous, vile, filthy, and disgusted.

I was only nine-year-old.

I remember being unable to walk and spending hours sitting on the cold ground. The winds were so strong and wild they pierced my fragile skin. I was bleeding but didn't know where it was coming from. Maybe I was bleeding from the inside. *Maybe my heart was bleeding,* I thought. I wanted to kill myself.

And I was only nine-year-old.

I remember my thoughts; Why me? What did I do to deserve that? Oh God, please tell me what I did. I'm sorry if I was a bad boy. I'm sorry I lied to my mom. Please God, why me?

I am only a nine-year-old kid.

I remember the walk back to my house. Full with shame and guilt. I was so heavy that each step felt like it was cracking the floor. I thought it was my fault. It must have been something I did. I remember the agony. I was in so much pain that it felt like wild dogs were feeding on me.

I was only nine-year-old.

I felt like I just survived drowning. I was wet and exhausted. And I stank of the smell of streets, dirt and filth. I looked and felt homeless.

I was too young to feel all that anguish.

I was only nine-year-old

when I was raped on my walk home from school.

28 Days Before He Shoots Himself

"Death and You"

I stink
of bad memories
and death.
And death
grabs me by the throat
not hard enough
to kill me.
I'm out of breath
as much as
I'm out of you.
I'm stuck
between death
and the memories
of you.

27 Days Before He Shoots Himself

"Not Getting Better"

"I don't remember much of it. I don't remember what happened. But mostly I remember the feeling."
I'm currently in Dr. Richard's office. It's cold and I'm trembling. Talking about that incident is the most difficult thing I have to do. But I have to talk about it because, as everyone says, it's all part of the healing process.
"Did you tell your parents about it?"
"I did tell my mother about it the next day. She burst out crying. I remember her telling me that it was my fault. I should have taken the bus instead. But I liked to walk." I tremble. "I felt bad for months after that since I didn't take the bus. I thought it was entirely my fault. I still believe it was my fault at times."
WHAT ARE YOU DOING HERE? YOU ARE NEVER GOING TO GET BETTER. THIS IS TOO MUCH FOR YOU. LEAVE.
"It's not your fault, Luke. It is never the victim's fault."
Was I truly a victim? Or maybe I did that to myself by not taking the bus.
YOU DID THAT TO YOURSELF. IT'S YOUR FAULT.
YOU WILL NEVER HEAL.
"What about your father?" He asks.
"My mother first warned me not to tell him because he would get furious. But he found out a few days later because the crying in the house was too much for him. When he found out, he told me that I wasn't a man enough, to begin with. He slapped me and blamed me for everything that had happened. He said that I should have spent more time playing football and less time reading. He prohibited me from leaving the house for nearly a year. Until we pretended the incident never happened."
Dr. Richard stops writing. He places his pen and notebook down on the table.
"Are you still in touch with your father?" He asks.

"He passed away a few years ago." My vision blurs as I struggle to keep my emotions at bay. "My father was never kind to me. That made me feel worse about the incident."

"Did they ever catch the monster who did that to you?"

"They didn't. Or they did. I don't know. I don't remember his face. He may be in jail. And he may be free. And it hurts."

"I'm sorry you had to go through that, and thank you for sharing your story with me. This will help with your progress."

The truth is that I'm not making any progress here. In fact, every time I see Dr. Richard, I feel like I'm getting worse. But I only come because everyone tells me that I should come here.
And also for the pills.
YOU WILL NEVER GET BETTER. DR. RICHARD WILL ONLY MAKE YOU FEEL WORSE.
WHAT IF HE TELLS SOMEONE ABOUT THE INCIDENT?
WHAT IF HE GIVES UP ON YOU?
HE WILL.
EVERYONE DOES.

Depression

Allow me to tell you a little bit more about Luke. His story has already come to an end, but it is about to begin anew. His life has been steeped in melancholy. And all will come to an end when he pulls the trigger.

Luke was a happy boy once. I wasn't there, but I can see him recall some vivid memories from his childhood. But his childhood was ended when a monster touched him. And I was introduced to Luke as his forever companion. I have been stuck with him since then. He sometimes tries to ignore me and walks away. But I'm always there, just out of sight.

What is he thinking right now as he points the gun to his head? I can tell you. He is terrified. Wouldn't you be? You'd think he'd be ready for death by now after so many years of darkness towering over his head. You would think, oh, Luke is brave to be holding a gun. But it isn't bravery that is driving him right now. Bravery is only meaningful to those who understand the difference between life and death.

And Luke is on the edge of both.

26 Days Before He Shoots Himself

"A Sad Place"

I am a victim;
a vest,
not aware of
the wreckage
it houses.

I was not like this before.
Once upon a time,
I fell in love
and that made my life
as easy as a breeze
and changed the ways
I cared about people.
Every hour of the day
became
a fresh,
new longing for
the early morning sun.

Your promises are
blurred images
you fail to recognize.

It all seemed easy to you
when you
ended me.
But It's not about the end,
it's about the power
in which these promises
outpoured.

I think the love
we hold for some people

resides in
the one leap of faith
the heart takes
on the sound of one of
the promises
you have yearned for a long time
to hear.

I loved you more,
every time you lied and yet,
what hurts the most was that
we were more
in love
with my idea of love
and my idea of you
than we ever actually were.

Here, everyone's in love
and yet, it's a sad place.

25 Days Before He Shoots Himself

"Be a Man"

My parents had always hated me. You believe that this is how most of us feel towards our parents, but this isn't my case. My father used to tell me *"I hate how soft you are"* and my mother used to say *"I wish you were more like your brother; you would have gotten along better with your father. It would have made everything easier in the house"*. I was always the forgotten at family dinners. The stigma. The disgrace of the family.

Things got worse for me after my incident. My parents both treated me as if I were invisible. I once overheard my father on the phone telling someone, "I have only one son, his name is Ryan," and my mother played along because she was afraid of my father. Following the incident, I was pronounced dead in the family.

My older brother, Ryan, is currently serving his time in jail for beating up his wife to death. Four years ago, he locked his wife up in the house and tortured her for days because he thought that she was cheating on him with her boss. He was condemned to fourteen years in prison.

"I wish you were more like your brother." My father said at our last supper together.

"Would you like me to be a murderer?" I said.

"Don't talk back at your father. He is sick." My mother defended her husband. She has never been able to tell the difference between love and fear.

"I want you to be a man." was the final thing my father said to me.

"I'm a man. I'm just not as cruel as you and Ryan." was the last thing I said to my father before he had a heart attack and passed away.

Depression

Luke has always felt unwanted, and it all started because of his father.

All of our insecurities stem from our parents. And his, too.

Yours too, right?

How many times did your parents make you hate yourself? How many times have they made you feel unwanted?

Back to Luke, he liked reading more than anything else in the world. And his father despised him for it. Books softened him. Made him kind and just. His father wanted a strong, athletic son. And the books couldn't help Luke become the man his father wanted.

Luke loathed himself for his inability to be loved by his father. So he continued to read books about other families. He imagined himself living inside one of his books until he was completely immersed in one of them; forgotten.

Luke's parents had also forgotten about him. They were so proud of Luke's brother, Ryan, that they began to mention Luke less and less. They no longer called him for dinner. They had stopped celebrating his birthday. Many times, Luke overheard his parents discussing his brother with others, and they never mentioned him.

And every time, he retreats to his room and cries himself to sleep.

He was

forgotten.

Unwanted.

24 Days Before He Shoots Himself

"Parents and Children"

Everyone talks about sons and daughters neglecting their parents, but no one talks about what parents do to their children. Nobody talks about the childhood emotional neglect caused by parents' failure to respond to their child's emotional needs. Nobody talks about how neglect can scar children for life and has long-term implications.

I suffered greatly as a child as a result of neglect and ignorance. Most of the time, I was depressed and lonely. Whenever I tried to open up or talk about my worries and troubles with my parents, all I got was a look that said I was acting like a child, when in reality I was just a child. I was seeking help, but my problems seemed small and insignificant to my parents. They may have been small, but so was I. Small problems are big problems for a young child. They were unconcerned about my problems. I was bullied a lot at school and had no one to tell, so no one was there to defend me. The only thing I could do was cry alone or swallow the entire burden and hold it all inside me for good.

What's the harm in wanting to be loved by my parents? Isn't that what every child wishes for? Isn't it natural for children to share their emotions with the ones they care about the most? If I cried, I was told to stop being childish and stop crying. I wasn't allowed to show my emotions if I was sad or upset, or else I'd be punished by ignorance. My parents were always judgmental and dismissive of my feelings. And when things went wrong in my life, all they could do was remind me that they provided a home with basic amenities and a decent life. But here's the thing: I didn't ask for this life. You brought me into this world, and I'm entirely your responsibility.

And I grew up with a heavy bag of emotional corruption inside me, running through my veins, generated and developed by my parents. I still believe that I am difficult to love and be loved. Still, I think that crying is unacceptable. And I'll always think there's something wrong with me because I feel too much.

And for anyone considering having children, if you believe you will be unable to meet your child's emotional needs, please do not have them.

23 Days Before He Shoots Himself

"Smoking Memories"

Dr. Richard advised me to write more about Harmony to get her out of my system completely.

"It's too soon to say goodbye to her entirely, but we'll take it one step at a time," he explained.

I know I'll never be able to get over her. She is etched in my brain's tissues for the rest of my life. And I will always enjoy writing about her. It reminds me of the warmth I used to feel when we were together.

What do you want me to tell you about Harmony Deadwood?

She was beautiful. The most beautiful woman I've ever met. And I felt so ugly around her. And I loved her. I still do. Three years together. One year of marriage. Lots of laughs and cries. Lots of smiles and frowns. We were extraordinary. I thought we were out of this world, until we suddenly weren't. We were flying together, and without warning, I found myself wandering alone. We were in love until I found out that I was the only one in love. The tragedy is that I'm still not sure where we went wrong. It just happened, like a long night after a beautiful day, natural and inevitable.

Having too many memories can be as bad for your heart as smoking. Every night, I inhale one memory and exhale another until my brain and lungs give out. And, thanks to Harmony's memories, I smoke a pack or two every day. The way she laughed with the tip of her tongue protruding from her mouth, the way she smells, her caramel curly hair always trying to cover her eyes. Her eyes and eyelashes looked more like a painting. Her hands, too. I adored her hands, especially how warm they were. And I fell in love with her vulnerabilities and the way she attempted to hide her imperfections from the rest of the world.

I loved her and sometimes the only mistake you make in a love story is loving someone with all your heart until it starts beating for them. And it stops beating for you. At the end of it all, you find yourself heartless.

It's weird how love sometimes can turn into nothing; a mountain into dust.

A rush of feelings and intimacy
into a void.
Null.
Nothing.

22 Days Before He Shoots Himself

"Writer"

It's been a while,
but you would say it's been forever.
There is a slight possibility
that you are thinking
of me.
Are you?
I still count
every sunrise,
every single one I witnessed
without you.
Though you didn't die,
your separation
feels forced
like death.

You know me,
I'm familiar with death.
I read you like my favorite book.
I know all of your secrets
and we know all about our Summer getaways
when I used to watch you
through the eyes of a man
who isn't me anymore.

I died
the second
you left.
And you lived.
And you lived.

Do you believe in resurrection?
Will you ever come back?

Same questions.
Same answers.

And I loved you
the way a
little girl
loves her flowers.
gentle,
curious,
and
oddly bittersweet.

But do you still love me?
Or has your heart turned to coal
that is waiting to be ignited
at the thought of me?

I used to be a writer,
but I can't write anymore.

I'm finished.

21 Days Before He Shoots Himself

"Fix Your Anxiety"

I had always thought that I'd be one of those people that finds love easy and settles down. I had always believed that each of us has a soulmate whom we will ultimately meet. I never received the love I thought I deserved from my parents, so I began to look for it elsewhere. I was certain of what I wanted, to find true love, and be loved in return.

And then I found Harmony, or maybe she found me. And my romantic fantasies, my visions, came true exactly as I had envisioned. The first time we touched, kissed or fought. Everything felt like it was a scene from a movie. And I was sincerely looking forward to my happy ending.

Two years later, our love was sealed with marriage. And, to be honest, it felt like the right thing to do at the time. I wanted nothing more than to spend the rest of my life with her. And the more love I gave, the more I received in return. Yes, I was happy. Really happy. But most importantly, I was *content*.

And then, suddenly, something changed, as if love had run out. We were out of sync. Something irreplaceable was lost. I'm still not sure what it was or when it happened. We did, however, lose something. She suddenly started seeing me clinging to her, and I suddenly started seeing her distant. She went out to see her friends more, and I wanted to spend more time with her.

"I feel like you're not yourself anymore," I said. "It's as though you've run out of love to give."

"For the love of God, Luke, get your anxiety under control." She yelled. "You are not my child; you are my husband. I'm not supposed to lavish you with love all the time. I can't give you the affection that your parents couldn't."

I warned her not to speak to me like that ever again. And she threatened to leave me. She showed less interest in me, and I worked harder to fix whatever was wrong between us. One fight led to another. Sunny days have turned into rainy days. Unstoppable rain, then storms. Then came the flood. We couldn't stop it anymore. We began to drown.

She wasn't my soulmate. She was my tormentor. She had had enough of me.

"I'm tired of you and your anxiety." She said. "I want to be with a real man who will look after me. I'm done looking after you."

"What exactly do you want me to do?" I asked helplessly.

"I want you to fix your anxiety," she said, crushing my heart.

I truly did everything I could to fix whatever was going on between us. I should have realized that some broken things are not meant to be repaired, especially when a piece is missing.

The missing piece was that she has fallen in love with someone else.

20 Days Before He Shoots Himself

"Toxic"

Being in a toxic relationship
feels like being constantly choked,
so close to death
but not strong enough to die.

She was killing me
and I was obsessed
with death.

20 Days Before He Shoots Himself

"Not Today"

There will come a day
when I will stop
burning myself
for you,
and instead,
I will burn
your photos
and memories
to
ashes.

A day will come
when I will stop
loving you.

But not today.

I will try
again
tomorrow.

19 Days Before He Shoots Himself

"I've Won"

How can someone
live outside
his head?

The little voice inside
my head is
getting louder.

I feel like my Depression
has grown a tongue
and started to talk to me.
Is that even possible?

I've reached the edges
that separate reality from delusions.
I can hear my Depression loud and clear.

"I've won." My Depression says.
"I've conquered you."
The voices are keeping me up all night
ringing in my ears.

There is no silence.
Only chaos
and pain.

Depression

Luke leaves nothing behind. No one will mourn him. No one will bury him. In a world full of filth and agony, he is forgotten dust in the wind. Hate and despair. Oh, what a cruel world filled with cruel people. There is nothing for him to go back to, and even worse, nothing to look forward to.

Can you hear him scream? Nobody can. However, I do. Every night, he screams different names and stories. Stories about lost lovers and bad habits. One love story ended in tragedy. A simple walk to school turned into a catastrophe.

He is in so much pain, alone in his room. The whole world neglects him. His fingers are on the verge of pulling the trigger.

PULL THE TRIGGER. JUST PULL IT. KILL YOURSELF. END YOUR MISERY. DO IT. DO IT. DO IT.

His soul is going to leave his body and travel into the unknown. He thinks that he is ready, but he is not.

Are you?

No one is ready for death.

Death yearns for life.

Death awaits,
and this is his
final destination.

18 Days Before He Shoots Himself

"The Day She Left"

I still remember holding onto this heavy thing inside my chest. Some call it love. Some call it abuse. I think it's like being inside a small room, and there isn't enough space for you to move. And you can't get around it. You can't see outside out of it. And then, at some point, the room becomes you.

I was a small room and Harmony was the whole house. It was mid-February when she had enough of me, and I had enough of fighting. I was barely breathing when she said, "You suffocate me."

"Sure, I will breathe less for you." And I held my breath for her. And I'd do it again, thousands of times over. I was madly in love. And we were in a sick Harmony.

"I can't do this anymore." was her reply when I asked, "How was your day?". She was constantly agitated. We were trying to have a baby, but it wasn't working, and it seemed like everything was my fault. And she hated me for it. She was looking for an excuse to leave me.

"I can't do this anymore."

"Neither do I, Harmony. I'm sick of you."

"Oh, you're sick of me? I'm the one who has to go through all of your struggles with your past, Depression, and anxiety."

"I'm sorry for my miserable past. I'm sorry I can't always show you my beautiful side all the time so you can stay in love with me."

And then I punched few walls. She also broke few things. Our screams got louder, and the neighbors thought we were going to kill each other. Until we were sick of fighting, she abruptly entered her bedroom and began gathering her belongings.

"Are you going to leave me?"

"This is something I should have done a long time

ago. There is no place for you in my life anymore, Luke."

I grabbed her wrists in an attempt to stop her.

"You're holding me accountable for things that happened to me. It's not my fault that I'm depressed. I didn't choose to be born with anxiety."

"It's your fault because you're weak," she said as she let go of my grip. "You could have fought this Depression, but you wake up wanting to be depressed every day."

"Do you believe I have a choice?"

"Luke, you always do."

She grabbed her belongings.

"Please don't leave me," I begged.

"You're pathetic, Luke. I'm in love with someone else. And it was you who made me fall in love with him because you couldn't love me enough."

I remember how I felt when she said that. Everything around her, including me, froze. But she didn't stop talking. "I was on pills because I could never have a child that will have your Depression. Your kids will be sick like you. And whatever it is that you are struggling with, it should die with you."

She then walked away. And everything unfroze.

The small room inside my chest was filled with water. I was drowning inside myself. My stone heart had fallen into oblivion, except for a few shards of hope that made me bleed every now and then. My laughter morphed into songs of sorrow.

She was gone.

And I was wrecked.

17 Days Before He Shoots Himself

"Decayed"

I can feel
my heart
getting ripped off
piece by piece.
Little by little.
It stretches out until it is cut
with every
wretched passing
day
like a slow
decay.

17 Days Before He Shoots Himself

"Enough"

I write the right words
for the wrong people
and give the wrong love
to the right people.

I write to be found
and end up lost
in cruelty
and neglect.

What is there to write?
What is there to live?

I shiver a little
every night
at the remorseless of time.

Tell me,
was I ever enough?

16 Days Before He Shoots Himself

"Kneel"

I've knelt thirty-four times since I was born. Each one was more meaningful than the one before it. I've burned every bridge that connected me to people.

I'm all alone now.

I smoked the devil out a long time ago. My pills are my food, and my air is agony. I'm stuck in the middle of this life, and I don't know how many days I have left, but I pray it's not many.

I've dated a lot of women, but just one of them has ever made me happy. I wanted to be with her till my last breath, but she decided to love someone else. I now have nothing but anecdotes about her written on scraps of paper. I could never write enough about her. I could kneel thirty-four more times and still, nothing would bring her back.

I'm completely lost, and that is the most exciting part about waking up. I have no one to love these days. And I have no one to love me. I'm in the arms of my Depression. I have no one to talk to, but I can now hear myself. I write in the hope that my words will reach whoever needs them. I'm not interested in saving myself, but my words might help someone else. I honestly don't know if I ever want to live anymore. She abandoned me, and when she did, she killed the guy I believed I was. Since then, I've been in and out of that grave, seeking redemption and forgiveness from everyone who would listen.

And I kneel one more time. I still love you. And I still hate you.

15 Days Before He Shoots Himself

"Waterfall"

We were happy.
Or I used to think that we were happy.
Few punches later,
she said, "I don't have a place in my life for you."
She didn't even stutter or
choke on her words.
She said the words as if they were the right words
to say
at the right time.
The words cascaded from her
beautiful lips
like a waterfall.
And birds stop singing
and the sky went red.
It was almost as if the world had
ended.
Except it hadn't.
I'm not yet dead,
but I'm beginning to feel at ease
in the grave she dug for me.

15 Days Before He Shoots Himself

"Between Two Lands"

On borrowed time,
you walked away
and stepped on me.

You left to the land of
the living
where the sun rises and sets
at your eyes every day.

You left me in the land of
the dead.

How have I slept
through the beauty
of your years
breathing your breath.

I was
losing myself
in your eyes
with no desire,
no intention,
of being found.

14 Days Before He Shoots Himself

"Life's Mockery"

Do you know how much I loved her? After everything she had done and said. After everything I had done and said. I loved her. And, to be perfectly honest, I still love her. Isn't that pathetic? The way love reveals our genuine frailty. Humans are nothing more than helpless creatures. We spend our lives attempting to get any type of power, whether via love, affection, or money. Any kind of power that would make it easier to hurt each other. Because all we do is bring each other harm. And if we don't destroy each other, we begin to destroy nature, animals, and all the other beautiful things in life.

A friend once told me that people have a habit of ruining beautiful things. It struck me as both poetic and sad. My friend was both poetic and sad. Fortunately, he killed himself.

Harmony caused me a great deal of pain. Wounds that go deeper than my bones; I'll be scarred for life as if I'd lost a leg. I sometimes believe that the only way for me to feel better is to hurt her back. But I can't do it. How can you hurt someone you genuinely love?

Do you know what the greatest mockery of life is? Everything you asked for will be given to you on a golden platter until you can't tell the difference between life and heaven. Until you reach a point where you begin to wonder what you did to earn all of this happiness, you might not be able to figure it out.

Then, all of a sudden, life takes everything you've been given. It also takes away some of the things you took for granted until you can't tell the difference between life and hell. And you begin to wonder what you did to deserve all of this pain.

13 Days Before He Shoots Himself

"Stray Cat"

I begged her
if she could accommodate me
in her
heart.
She said there was
no place for me
in her life
anymore.
And I would have settled
for a tiny corner.
I would have slept
on the cold floor
without a pillow,
next to her old shoes
and abandoned belongings.
I'd have slept on her porch
like a stray cat and
eaten her leftovers.
I would have settled
for less
and less,
but she said
there was
no place for me
in her life
anymore.

13 Days Before He Shoots Himself

"Brains and Lungs"

Sometimes I say
that the problem is with
my brain.
But mostly I think the problem
is with
my lungs.
They choke,
and they ache
for death
and how they pine
over your breath
and how they
torture me
over your absence

My life,
my death,
you left me breathless.

13 Days Before He Shoots Himself

"The Party"

"Where were you last night?" John, one of my colleagues, asks.

I give him the nod.

"You didn't show up to the party. It was legit. We missed you."

I nod once more.

We missed you.

Who are you? And why did you miss me?

People keep tossing words around, hoping to fit in and be accepted in this cult called life.

We could have saved the world if we only knew how to express our feelings in the right places and to the right people.

"And you really missed a lot. Tresha made out with the weird accountant from the third floor. And there was also a hot tub. The party was alive man."

"I missed a lot, yes, I was in my room alone with a 1912 typewriter, whose maker died a long time ago. I was listening to Bach, who died in 1750. Then I watched a movie for Heath Ledger, who died in 2008. Then, before going to bed, I read Charles Bukowski, who died in 1994. I was surrounded, beautifully, by death. Believe me, John, I have never felt more alive."

John stares back at his computer.

And so the day goes on.

12 Days Before He Shoots Himself

"Yes, She Is"

I don't think Dr. Richard has made me feel any better. I'm trying to contact friends for help, but they're ignoring me. No one can handle my darkness, and most of them are terrified of me as if my Depression is contagious.

I'm trapped in a loop where I have to go to a job I despise and then return to my cold, lonely home. I don't have much time for anything else because I spend most of my time at the hospital with my mom. We've been looking for a kidney donor for a long time, and I'm starting to lose hope.

YOU WILL NEVER FIND A DONOR. YOUR MOTHER WILL DIE.

My mind is too loud. I wish there was a way to turn it off. I wish I could confide in my mother, but we don't have that type of relationship. I love my mother to death, but I don't believe she feels the same way about me. I feel like she still blames me for my father's death. She never mentioned it, but I could tell how she refers to him as if he was the victim.

IT'S YOUR FAULT. YOU KILLED YOUR FATHER. YOUR MOTHER BLAMES YOU FOR THAT. SHE NEVER LOVED YOU.

"Have you seen Ryan?" She asks as soon as she sees me. She constantly asks about my brother Ryan before she asks whether I'm doing good. SHE LOVES RYAN IN WAYS THAT SHE COULD NEVER LOVE YOU.

"No, mom, I'm extremely busy with work," I explain as I prepare her dinner.

"Oh, my God, I miss him so badly. Please tell him that." She bursts into tears. "I can't believe I might never see him again."

"Please, don't say that, Mom. We'll find a donor soon NO SHE WON'T and you'll be as tough as a mountain."

I say, holding her hands. Even if we have a donor, I don't think I can afford it. I might have to sell the house.

"Go to your brother," she is shivering with tears. "Ask if they can let him out to see his dying mother."

"You are not dying, mom."

Yes, she is.

ATTA BOY.

11 Days Before He Shoots Himself

"Ryan Adams"

"My mother wants to see you," I tell my brother.

He's seated across from me in the jail visitors' room, which stinks of piss and vomit. It's deafeningly loud, and the air is thick with violence and cruelty. BE CAREFUL, LUKE. SOMETHING BAD MIGHT HAPPEN TO YOU. BE CAREFUL. Ryan is staring at me with disdain. He is not pleased to see me. We were never really close. He is arrogant, harsh, and selfish, much like my father. And he's been bitter his entire life. Thank you, Mom and Dad, for spoiling him.

"What do you want, Luke?" He asks.

"Your mother is dying," I say, raising my voice to seem tough. He's always intimidated me, and I've always felt small in his presence. "I don't want anything from you. My mother simply wishes to see you. Speak with the warden. See if you can get some sort of permission to see her."

"Who told you I want to see her?" With a frigid voice and a malicious smirk, he says. After all these years, I still can't believe he's my brother. I can't believe how vicious he's turned out to be.

"You know... I've always wished she loved me the way she loves you," I say as I stare into his piercing eyes, full of madness.

"I'm not sure how you can stand this woman. She watched our father repeatedly beating both of us to death and did nothing to stop it." His voice expresses a variety of emotions, anger and hatred. "I'm locked up because of her. Because I grew up in a sick house."

"No, Ryan, you're in here because you almost killed your wife to prove to yourself that you're a man," I yell.

"What do you know about being a man?" He says this with a half-smile. Wickedly pleased.

There is silence. My words are stuck in my throat. I shouldn't have played with the devil.

LUKE, GET OUT BEFORE HE HURTS YOU. SOMETHING TERRIBLE IS ABOUT TO HAPPEN. LEAVE. LEAVE. LEAVE.

"You lost your manhood the night you were raped." He keeps laughing like a lunatic. "Tell me, brother, did you enjoy it? Are you still daydreaming about that night?" Needles to my ears. I feel like my throat is closing.

YOU ARE GOING TO HAVE A HEART ATTACK. YOUR LUNGS ARE NOT WORKING. DO SOMETHING. ARE YOU GOING TO DIE? IS HE GOING TO HURT YOU?

My anxiety is out of control, and my eyes are on fire. I'm having trouble breathing.

YOU ARE UNABLE TO BREATHE. YOU'RE GOING TO PERISH. NOBODY CARES ABOUT YOU. EVERYONE DESPISES YOU. EVEN YOUR OWN FAMILY DESPISES YOU. YOU ARE ENTIRELY UNLOVABLE.

I get to my feet and gather my strength. "I hope you rot in prison, and if not, I pray you will rot in hell," I say.

I receive a text message.

I want to see you.

I miss you.

from Harmony.

Depression

A dream, of what's to come, or of what was of him. Poor Luke. How insignificant he is in comparison to what he is feeling. Weak and pathetic. Small and withered. He crumbles if anyone mentions the incident. It's been years, but for him, it feels like it happened yesterday. He is still that kid who was neglected by a world full of monsters. I can tell he's been consuming himself by his pain. He believes that by helping his sick mother, he will be helped. He believes there is yet hope for him. Nobody can help him. Once I have you in my grasp, I will never let you go. The pain does not bargain. It shows no mercy. It is devoid of logic. It is eternal. And now that it's taken hold, it'll latch to his body and head until there's nothing left of him. Until what's left of him is conquered by death.

Luke's death will be a travesty. His entire life will be for naught.

It's only a matter of time. Soon, he'll be able to do what he's wanted to do since the day of the incident.

10 Days Before He Shoots Himself

"She is Back"

Let's meet at my house, tomorrow at 6:00 PM.

I replied to Harmony. And I'm here waiting. My heart is racing against the clock. It's nearly 6:00 p.m. and Harmony is missing me. We'll get together again. And I, too, shall be saved. She is going to save me.

I jump to open the door when she knocks. This is the end of the story, and the beginning. This is the moment I've been looking forward to. We are going to get back together. BE CAREFUL. SOMETHING TERRIBLE IS ABOUT TO HAPPEN.

She's right there. She doesn't look like the way I sewed her to my memories. She is more beautiful. It's been about six months since I last saw her. She runs over to hug me. Home, this feels like home. I hold her closer, like a child holding his mother. And I start to heal.

RUN, LUKE. RUN.

"I heard about your mom," she says, still hugging me, "and I hope you find a donor soon."

I don't respond to her. In a moment like this, words are meaningless compared to emotion.

We sit for hours on end. And I tell her about the agony that is consuming me. I tell her about Ryan and my mom. I tell her about Dr. Richard and how hard I'm working on getting over her and moving on with my life. She hasn't said a word, but I can feel her gaze communicating with me. We are sitting on the couch, in front of the fireplace, and clasping hands. This reminds me of the good old days when we were happy.

"May I spend the night?" She asks. And I feel like I'm being resurrected. SAY NO, LUKE. SHE IS GOING TO DESTROY YOU.

"Of course," I answer her.
I take her hand in mine and kiss it.
And then she kisses me.
It's heaven on earth.

SHE IS ONLY GOING TO HURT YOU, LUKE.
WHY ARE YOU DOING THIS TO YOURSELF?

10 Days Before He Shoots Himself

"Addictions"

Love wrecks me
every time
and I always
go back
for more.

It's our addictions
to self-destructions
and our longing for
death
and all the other
beautiful things
that comes along.

9 Days Before He Shoots Himself

"Never You"

Dreams collide with reality. Harmony is by my side when I wake up. This isn't a dream. This is my new reality. This is heaven on earth.

She wakes up.

"Good morning," I greet.

"I longed for the days when I could wake up next to you." She says this while running her finger across my cheek.

"Would you like to move in with me again?" I ask her.

She gives me an odd, familiar look.

"Oh, Luke, you misunderstood me. I'm still in love with Sammy. I'm still with him."

I can feel all of my blood coursing through my veins and rushing to my head. I feel like my throat is shutting. OH, LUKE WHAT HAVE YOU DONE?

I get out of bed. I need to get away from her. I feel like I'm about to puke.

"Wait, Luke, what did you expect? You know how much I love Sammy." SHE IS GOING TO HURT YOU. LEAVE. DO SOMETHING.

"Why did you come here?" I yell at her. I'm boiling with rage. I feel like I'm going to be shattered into small little shards.

"I came here to support you. I've heard you're going through a lot."

She climbs out of bed, grabs my face, and kisses me once more.

I push her away. I feel sick.

IT'S ALL YOUR FAULT.

"What exactly are you doing, Harmony? What is this sick game you're playing here?"

"I miss you, Luke. I miss the beautiful things you used to give me. But I'm also madly in love with Sammy. However, he's not you."

She is sick. SHE IS SICK.

"Get out of the house," I say.

KICK HER OUT BEFORE SHE HURTS YOUR MORE.

She is taken aback.

"GET OUT OF THE HOUSE," I say again.

"Oh my God, you are pathetic," she says as she begins to grab her belongings. "You know I've never loved you? I tried, but you're just so unlovable. I just loved the idea of you." With each word she says, I feel myself descending from the heavens to the bottom. "You get a tiny amount of attention and mistake it for love."

LUKE, SHE NEVER LOVED. YOU ARE COMPLETELY UNLOVABLE. YOUR LIFE COMES TO AN END HERE. NOBODY CARES ABOUT YOU. YOU ARE WORTHLESS.

"You are worthless," she screams as she opens the door.

I'm following her to make sure she leaves, this time for good.

"I've only ever loved the things you've given me, never you." She says before slamming the door.

And I can hear my heart cracking to smithereens by now.

SHE USED YOU. SHE ALWAYS DID. SHE NEVER LOVED YOU.

DO SOMETHING.

DO SOMETHING.

DO SOMETHING.

I HAVE AN IDEA...

DO YOU HAVE A GUN?

There is something
you must never forget

if you ever decide to
leave someone,

please
don't
you
ever
come
back.

You will only
kill them
twice.

8 Days Before He Shoots Himself

"Late Night Sadness"

There's a taste in my mouth
bitter as my days.
It smells like
desperation everywhere.
And rain.
And sadness.

We shouldn't have ended like this.
And winter shouldn't have stayed
this long.

I'm lost between sadness
and you.

I don't like
myself anymore.
You were the best part
of me.

I feel so many things
towards myself.
Detest.
Blame.
Hatred.
Aversion.

I hate being alive,
and I still love you.

8 Days Before He Shoots Himself

"Death by Words"

I died
the day the words
"I love you."
died on your lips.

Bleeding on the floor,
my cracked ribs
reformed grotesquely
as I turn and twist
to the words
that ring in my ears.
"I've never loved you."

You killed me
and still
it's your ghost
that
haunts me.

7 Days Before He Shoots Himself

"Hunger"

Moments eat moments.
Now, these days, I'm quiet about you.
It almost feels like I forgot you but I never will.

People want to hear about love all the time
but they don't want to hear about tragedies.

We were toxic and
you never loved me.

And I tried to search for some answers
to questions that don't make sense to anyone.

I was desperately hoping that
I would prove my doubts wrong.

I knew you didn't love me,
and you had no intention to,
but I was so deeply in love with you,
and I don't think I can be blamed for
loving you.

It's not my fault,
nor is it yours.

There are no victims of love
because it's something we can't control.

You couldn't love me,
and I couldn't stop loving you.

Love is as inevitable as death.
And love can lead to death sometimes.
Sometimes.

6 Days Before He Shoots Himself

"Cyclone"

Love can swallow us like
a cyclone.
Madness
and screams.
Aching
and sweats.
Stories are written on our skin forever.
And that's the only meaning
of forever,
in love.
The pain,
the ache,
the memories.
Everything else fades away
the love,
the lust.

Your greatest love story is
waiting to be consigned
to darkness.

5 Days Before He Shoots Himself

"March"

Do you remember the third of March?
I didn't want anything
else
I only wanted you.
But now I want anyone
to torture and hurt
me
like I deserve
to be hurt.
I want anyone to numb
this feeling
of agony and pain
like I don't deserve
to feel.

There's this thought I get
every now and then,
the slight possibility
that I deserve to be treated badly
because I'm nothing.
I'm ugly.
I'm fat.
I'm nothing.

5 Days Before He Shoots Himself

"Him"

There is a knock on the door. Then there is the second. I'm sick of this cold, empty huge house. I'm using again. Things to keep my mind off the ground. These knocks could be hallucinations. I hear more knocks on the door. This time it's harder. My heart starts beating faster.

I can't hear my anxiety anymore. The pills are working.

Something isn't quite right. It's almost midnight; who is coming to see me now? Maybe they'll go away if I just ignore them.

The knocks get harder. I try to get up. I'm exhausted and dizzy. I make myself stand up. I open the door as soon as I get to it.

"Luke!" A middle-aged man who appears to recognize me and acts as though he knows who I am. I'm getting a prick in my stomach. He sounds incredibly familiar, like if he was an old acquaintance. Is he a friend or foe?

"Do I know you?" I inquire, breathing deeply into the cold December air. I'm feeling sick.

"You don't know who I am, but..." he struggles to find the perfect words to say. "I did all the tests in the hospital, and they confirmed I was a match," he nervously touches his face. He's trembling. "I can give a kidney to your mother..." He takes a cautious pause. "... my kidney."

I feel like my heart is pumping so much blood to all of my organs that I'm about to pass out. I can hear my anxiety speaking to me once more. WHAT'S HAPPENING? WHO IS THIS? THIS MAN IS GOING TO HURT YOU. WHY DID YOU OPEN THE DOOR? YOU ARE AN IDIOT, LUKE. I'm not sure who this man is, but I feel like I want to throw up. DON'T BREATHE.

"Why are you going to do that?" I ask, completely perplexed. I have the impression that this is all a figment of my imagination. Something doesn't feel right. I feel sick. DON'T BREATHE.

Oh god, what's wrong with me? I feel really, really sick. YOU KNOW THIS MAN. THIS MAN IS YOUR ENEMY,

"Luke," he repeats my name. I'm having trouble remembering who he is, as if my brain is stopping me from doing so. "I just want you to know how sorry I'm for what I did to you."

It's him. IT'S HIM. It's him. It's him. IT'S HIM. RUN LUKE! RUN!!

"I'm married now. I have a beautiful wife and two lovely children. I'm sorry for what I did to you. I was young and naive. I want you to forgive me."

"Stop talking." I'm feeling dizzy and out of breath. I can't take it anymore. I can hardly stand. DON'T BREATHE. YOU SHOULD HAVE ENDED YOUR MISERY. YOU CAN'T HANDLE ALL OF THIS PAIN. KILL YOURSELF.

"Listen to me, Luke."

"Stop ... talking." I'm having a panic attack. I feel like my heart is going to stop. YOUR HEART IS GOING TO STOP.

"If I could go back in time, I would have taken it all back. I was sick. I worked on myself, and I was healed. I'm better now."

"Stop. Please."

"I looked you up months ago to make sure you were okay after what I did to you. And I just saw you the other day; you're successful and in good health. It made me happy. As if I haven't harmed you. You're doing well. You are whole."

"Please.... Please stop." I barely can talk anymore, and he's not going away. I place my hand on my heart. It hurts. It hurts. YOU ARE HAVING A HEART ATTACK.

"I recently heard about your mother and felt this would be an excellent opportunity for me to make amends and to put the past behind us.."

"Make ... amends?"

"Yes, I will do whatever you want."

"I want you to ... leave."

"Please, listen to me. I'm sorry. I feel terrible about what I did to you. The guilt is eating me alive. I don't deserve this. You don't deserve this either. Please forgive me so that I can be free of you. And you will be free of me as well. I don't want your karma to hurt my children. I don't want my children to go through what you've gone through."

"You ... are a monster."

"I used to be. But I've changed."

"You ruined me."

"I understand. But I'm here to make things right."

"Make things right? Are you out of your mind? I can't be fixed. You ruined me. You left me there, bleeding to death. You are a filthy animal and you will always be. And I'll never forgive you because what you did to me is unforgivable." My heart is about to stop. IT WILL STOP. THIS MAN WILL KILL YOU. RUN.

"I want you to listen to me. I will fix you. I promise."

"Leave, please," I whisper. I can't breathe now, and his words are choking me even more.

"I've completed all of the necessary medical tests and I'm ready to donate my kidney to your mother. Don't squander this chance because of an old grudge. Think about your mother."

"You ruined me..." I exhale, attempting to catch my breath. "You ruined me, and I can't forgive you even if you offer your filthy soul to my mother."

I collapse to the ground, a much-needed fall that I wish would be the death of me.

And I think,

oh sweet death.

You are so beautiful.

You are so beautiful.

You are so beautiful.

YOU ARE READY.

Depression

What would you do in Luke's situation? He is engulfed in darkness. His past appears to be a carbon copy of his future. Pale and gloomy. Everyone had deserted him. But I'm still here. I'll always be there for him. I'll watch after him and make sure he has a safe journey to whatever awaits him after this life.

No one can tolerate the level of pain he is experiencing. No one deserves to suffer this way. He is paralyzed with melancholy. He is crippled by sadness. No one deserves this, not even you. Yes, I'm talking to you, the one reading this from your comfortable couch. What do you know about pain? What do you know about loneliness? Probably nothing. No one has ever endured as much as Luke. My Luke. I will help in putting an end to his agony once and for all.

There isn't much more to his story. His adventure is coming to an end. And so is his brief existence. He only has a few words to say and a few steps to take before this is all over.

Are you ready for his end?

Are you ready for yours?

4 Days Before He Shoots Himself

"Hospitals"

White walls.
White sheets.
White curtains.
Death awaits.
The smell of sulfur and piss.
The old man is crying for help.
The newborn is crying for help.
It's chaos between life and death.
The morgue and the nursery
are few feet apart.
White coats.
White blankets.
White halls.
The living wants to live longer
and the dead won't hear us.
We try to live,
almost.
We try to die,
almost.
It's chaos between
right and wrong.

4 Days Before He Shoots Himself

"Same"

People ask me if
I wish you
bad things
or I wish you well.
The truth is
that
I wish you
nothing
but the same pain
you gave me.
The same
ache in my heart.
The same
sleepless night.
The same
agony.

Just
the
same.

3 Days Before He Shoots Himself

"It's Time"

"What do you remember?"

I have no recollection of what happened. I'm in a hospital bed, wired up to machines. I remember feeling a sharp pain in my chest. I remember the agony of seeing the man who killed my childhood. I remember him killing me once more.

"I remember having a heart attack," I explain.

"Because many of the symptoms are similar, many people who suffer from panic attacks wrongly feel they are suffering from a heart attack." The doctor says.

"But, it felt..." I'm struggling to catch my breath. "It felt real."

"Both conditions can be accompanied by shortness of breath, tightness in the chest, sweating, a pounding heartbeat, dizziness, and even physical weakness or temporary paralysis." He puts his notes away. "We have completed all of the examinations, and you are free to leave after a few more quick tests. You don't need to be concerned."

The doctor leaves and two nurses enter to take my blood pressure and unplug the machines attached to my chest.

"Your mother," says the blonde nurse. "Your mother is tired, Luke. You should go check on her."

And I know.
It is time.

2 Days Before He Shoots Himself

"Goodbye"

"I'm sorry, Luke; I've not been a good mother to you." I'm clutching my mother's icy hand. Her room now smells like death. It's time.

"I forgive you. I forgive you." I'm crying like a little kid. The kid that she never let me be.

"You have been the most wonderful son I could have ever wished for. I regret not being a better mother to you. I wish I had spent more time with you that night. There is nothing I could say to make things better right now. If I could go back in time, I would do things differently for you."

She coughs and grips my hands even more tightly.

"You should know, Luke, that mothers feel things in mysterious ways. I loved you both the same, you and Ryan. But you have always been so hard to love. But I tried. As God is my witness, I tried. And I wished your father would try with me as well, but he always saw you as the soft one. And he saw Ryan as the strong one. Little did he know that you were much stronger, Luke. You have been fighting this disease. This thing you call Depression, for a long time. And years ago we didn't know much about it. I didn't know much about it. You are way stronger than everybody thinks."

I'm still crying and don't think I'll be able to stop. I kiss her on the cheek, cold and frail. "Please don't leave me, Mom. I'm not ready to face the world on my own."

"You certainly are, my dear. Luke, you will have a happy and long life, and you will find what you are looking for. You'll find out what aches you one day."

"I'm sorry, Mom. I'm sorry." Please do not leave me. Please."

"When we are alive, we don't appreciate life much. However, as death approaches, we tighten our grip on life. I wish I could spend more time with you. Nothing would make me happier than to stay with you for a few more years. And to see you marry the woman you love. And see your children. I wish I could."

I cry uncontrollably. And she cries with me too.

"I love you, Luke."

She says as death enslaves her soul.

"I love you too, mother."

Goodbye.

I don't want to end my
life now.
But I believe that
I'm going to die
either way
from loneliness and
heartbreak.

I don't want to go.
I don't want to go.
But it's time to leave.

Life is adjourned
and death is waiting.

1 Day Before He Shoots Himself

"You Chose Not To"

Depression, like an old friend, always finds its way back to me. I can't take it anymore, and there's no way out of this life cycle. Wake up, pretend to be someone you are not, repeat. Pretentious life filled with pretentious people. I don't belong with them. I'll never do. I want to scream at everyone, "I'm depressed," but I'm afraid they'll think I'm desperate for attention. Maybe I am.

The last time I opened up to a friend about my Depression, he said, "You are high maintenance and I can't be your friend anymore." It's sad and lonely to be living with a disease that no one else is aware of. Depression isolates you from the rest of the world and makes you feel so alone that you want to shoot yourself in the head to end it. That's right, I said it. I would have battled it if you had been there, but everyone chose to leave me alone to battle my demons. And the reality is, I'm too weak to fight my demons alone. My demons are ferociously powerful. And I'm too lonely to be alive.

Isn't it easier to have fake friends than to have depressed ones? Shallow, pretentious conversations, long, useless rides, and smoking various narcotics to distract you from the fact that your existence is meaningless. All of this is far less difficult than supporting a friend suffering from Depression.

Some people believe that Depression is contagious. Others believe you're dramatic. Others believe it is incurable.

No matter what you think
always remember that
you could have helped,
but you chose not to.

The Day He Shoots Himself

"One Shot"

My phone vibrates.
Mom is calling.
I switch off the phone.
It's all her fault. I think. I'm here, writing this, because of her, because she left me. Why did she leave me?
Hello mother, can you help me now? Or is it too late for me to be helped?
NO ONE CAN HELP YOU NOW. YOU ARE HOPELESS. DO IT.
I swallow more pills. Nothing seems to be numbing the ache I feel inside my guts. The pills got used to me like an old friend now, what a disgrace I've become. I'm in hate with myself and my body. I'm at my lowest. I don't think I'm human anymore. I descended from being human a long time ago. I'm a monster. I have never been this low. *Or have I?*
THIS IS YOUR LOWEST POINT. THERE IS ONLY ONE WAY OUT OF IT. DO IT. DO IT.
I'm in so much pain; not even all the pills in the world could make me feel better. I'm done with the unfairness of this world. I'm tired of being broken by something that happened years ago. The truth is, this isn't a decision that I've just made. I have been planning this day for a long time now. I was simply living for my mother. And since she's gone. I need to be gone too.
YES. DO IT. DO IT. DO IT.
My phone vibrates again.
DON'T ANSWER THE PHONE.
I try to focus and read the caller ID.
It's Dr. Richard.
Are you okay? He sends a text.
I'm sorry. I reply and switch off the phone.
YOU ARE READY.

I chose the way I want to die. I don't want to swallow enough pills that may fail to terminate me. I don't want to throw myself out of the window because I don't want to feel any more pain. I bought a gun a few weeks ago, and I thought a bullet to my brain would do it, an easy yet poetic death.

A BULLET TO THE BRAIN IS YOUR BEST OPTION.

The bright side is that I won't be here to clean the mess I will leave. For the first time ever, I won't be cleaning my mess nor anyone's anymore.

I'm curious when they'll find my body. YOU WILL ROT. Or who. THAT'S NOT IMPORTANT. FOCUS. I should be scared now. But I'm not. I'm somehow relieved that it will all be over in few moments. No more pain. No more anxiety. No more Depression. I will end it all with me.

I grab the gun, point it to my head. My hand starts to shake.

I'm not scared.

DO IT.

Goodbye, filthy ugly world.

Hello, beautiful empty death.

I pull the trigger.

His soul is in transition.
But his withered body remains.
Do you feel it too?
Death feels like crossing
into another world
that looks the same
but feels different.
Heaven or hell,
death is still
the same.

What comes after death?
It's probably nothing. We close our eyes and then darkness. And then nothing.
No fear. No yesterday. No tomorrow.
Just nothing.
Emptiness. Silence. Peace.
The peace that we dream of when we are alive.
No wars. No money. No borders.
Everything is merged to create a huge white canvas.
Null. Nothing.
You end everything the moment you die.
So, you better be ready.
Are you ready?

Part Two

OTHER BEAUTIFUL THINGS

World War III is a war
among ourselves.
We have the ability to help one another,
yet we choose not to.

We've been through a hard winter.
But winter has come to an end,
and so has our love.

The winds were wild
and so was our love.

The sky is beautiful
and so was your smile
when you used to tell me
about your day.

Hello,
I'm dead now.
It's time for my funeral.

I wish I was unforgetabble
like the sun
like the moon
like you.

Who am I?

Am I dead?

Is this how it feels to be dead?

I feel ... nothing.

I'm feeling lighter.

I feel as if I'm floating. I've finally arrived. I've reached the end of the line. The null point. The nothing.

I'm nothing now.

All of the agony, all of the memories, both good and terrible, are gone. I'm no longer enslaved by my suffering. I can't see anything, yet I get a sense of lightness. The air around me is fresh. I feel as though I'm sleeping on a cloud.

I still can't believe I did it. Everything is now gone. My Depression. My anxiety. My pain.

I'm free. I'm happy.

I'm alone...

Where is my mom?

MOM!

Mother!!

MOM!

I can't seem to find her. I can't see. Do we lose our sight when we die? It's all darkness.

I'm in a hole.

It's cold. I feel very cold.

Wait, why am I feeling? I'm dead and the dead don't feel. I want my mother. Where is my mother? What is this smell? I'm cold. I'm very cold. Can anyone hear me? I'm scared. Help me!!

Where am I? Where are my eyes? I'm trying to open them but I can't feel my eyes on my face. I feel like I want to wake up but I can't. Can anybody help me?

I'm hearing things. Murmuring. My ears are working.

"Nurse, I believe he is waking up." I overhear someone says.

Wait. She is talking to a nurse. Why is she talking to a nurse? Am I dreaming? Am I still alive?

"He has a heart rate of more than 120 beats per minute. Yes, I believe he is awakening."

What's happening? Help me, please. I feel like I'm falling. Please, someone help me.

"I'm curious what color his eyes are."

"Infinity, go to your room."

Can anybody hear me?

"I'm not in the mood to go to my room. I want to meet the guy who wasted his life for probably nothing, while some of us here are battling for our lives every day."

"Infinity, please leave if you are not going to be supportive. I'm trying to help the man."

Help. Please, help me.

"I will stop talking. But I won't leave."

My heart is pounding furiously. I'm feeling a variety of emotions. I feel like I'm falling from a mountain and rising from a deep hole at the same time. Wait, I can feel my chest. I can feel my face. My mouth. My tongue.

"He's twitching his lips."

"Does he want to say something?"

"What color are his eyes?"

"Infinity, please leave the room."

"All right, I'll stop."

My eyes. I can feel my eyes, but I can't open them.

"His eyes are moving; I'm going to call his doctor. Infinity, stay here and be nice."

"I will try."

I try to open my eyes once more. I feel like they're stuck. It's so bright, the light is hurting my eyes.

"Nurse, hurry up; he is waking up."

My eyes are dry, and opening them stings. I want to say something, but I can't find my voice. I want to see but It's blurry. Someone has their gaze fixed on me. A female. *Who is she?*

I take a deep breath, like the one we take after spending a long period underwater.

"Your eyes are blue. Like the ocean." The girl says.

"Who are you? Where am I"? I say. My throat is very dry and hurting.

"Welcome to heaven." She says.

Depression

WHAT HAPPENED?
Luke is meant to be dead, how come he is still alive? I can sense him small and withered. Needy like a little child. He should have ended. He did not. What is there for him? Why is he so enslaved to this life of torment and pain? What does remain of him to be given? He is a hollow man. He is devoid of anything. I don't understand.

But don't be concerned. Death will eventually gather all of the lost souls. I'll follow Luke like a shadow throughout the rest of his voyage. I'll assist him as I always have. And he'll listen to me like he always has. He won't be around for long since death will always collect. One night, he will abandon his world once more to follow in his mother's footsteps, to go to a place where the darkness cannot reach him.

This is not a triumph. When it comes to the darkness, there is no victory. He's just not dead...yet. Death will gnaw at him, biding his time. Death will only strike to kill Luke when he is at his weakest.

Look at him. He is surrounded by strangers pretending to care about him.

Will they be able to save him?

Can you save him?

No one can.
Not even you.
You'll see.

2 Days After He Shot Himself

"The Lucky"

"You're lucky, your hand couldn't withstand the gun's pushing force. You missed the shot, and the bullet barely scraped the top of your head." Dr. Richard says as he sits on a white chair across from my bed.

I'm still in *shock*.

"You passed out as a result of the trauma. You thought you were shot. I went straight to your place after receiving your text message." He is hesitant. "Your skull was splattered with blood. I hated myself because I thought you were dead. But then I checked your pulse and found out you were still alive." He takes a breather. He is looking at me as if I'm some kind of miracle. "You are still alive. All of the blood came from the bullet scratch. Luke, you are incredibly lucky."

"Lucky? Are you serious, Doctor?" I scream angrily. My throat is still dry, and my voice is barely audible and can't match my rage. "I'm still here; that means my pain is still here. My Depression is still here. My anxiety is still here. All my battles are yet to be fought. And I don't want to fight."

"It's never going to be easy, Luke. Those demons that torment you must be subdued. And you must be strong enough to keep them under control. Mental illness is a war. And you continue to lose battles but not the war. You're still alive which means you still have a fighting chance. And I'm here to help you."

"When will I be able to leave the hospital?" I inquire.

"Not yet," he says as he stands up, "You will stay here for a few days under my supervision. Until your head heals fully and I make sure that you will be alright."

"But I want to go."

"Luke, you are a risk to yourself. And I'm not going to let you hurt yourself again. I need you to help me to help you."

3 Days After He Shot Himself

"Slow Death"

Sometimes
you survive
but you don't actually
survive.
You don't belong to
anyone,
not to yourself even.
You are not
dead.
You are not
alive.
You exist.

And the truth is
that is not
actually
surviving;
that's a slow death.

4 Days After He Shot Himself

"Trying to Die"

"You must eat," advises the nurse. "It will help your recovery." Her name is Sandy and she's very sweet. And I'm exhausted.

Do I want to get better and return to a life I worked so hard to escape?

"I'm going to leave you now, but promise me you'll eat something."

"I promise," I say. And I don't mean it.

"He is lying, he won't eat." The same girl that was here when I woke up enters my room. She is around my age and based on the robe she's wearing, I'm assuming she's a patient here. Her skin is white, nearly translucent, and practically gleaming.

"Infinity, Leave him alone and go to your room. You should lay down after your treatment." Sandy says.

Her name is Infinity. I heard the nurse calling her many times when I was trying to wake up. *Was she here the whole time I was asleep?*

"I'll just say hi to Blue Eyes and walk away." She tells Sandy.

She looks tired and sick, but she's trying way too hard to keep it hidden. Her hospital robe appears to be worn. Her head is obscured by a red scarf, making her skin appear paler.

She walks around my room, inspecting all of the food I haven't eaten. I'm feeling exposed. "You ought to eat, Blue Eyes."

"My name is Luke," I say, irritated. I hate my blue eyes.

"I know. Luke Adams." She repeats my name like she practiced saying it many times before.

"How do you know my name?" I ask. "And who are you?"

"My name is Infinity. I'm a patient here." She says.

"Cancer patient, if you're wondering, which is why I'm wearing a scarf over what's left of my hair." She points to her scarf. "I kept an eye on you and cared for you while you slept after you tried to kill yourself."

She knows. Everybody knows.

I feel naked. I feel I'm getting sick.

WHO IS SHE? WHAT DOES SHE WANT FROM YOU?

Infinity sits on the chair opposite my bed. "I was also talking to you every day. Did you hear me?"

"You have a beautiful name, Infinity. What is your surname?" I inquire, attempting to dodge her question.

"Other beautiful things." She says sarcastically. She moves her chair closer to me. "Please tell me," she pleads. "Did you hear me when I was talking to you?"

I hesitate to answer. I don't know what I remember. My memory is very foggy, and I can still hear the gunshot. "No," I reply. "I heard nothing."

She looks at me, then up to the ceiling. She is disappointed. "Do you believe there is life after death, Luke Adams?" She inquires.

"Well, I didn't die, Infinity *'Other Beautiful Things'*. You know that already, don't you?" I say fretfully.

"I understand. But, since you tried to end your own life, I figured you'd at least be aware of what awaits us beyond death."

I don't believe I'm prepared to have this conversation. I don't want to talk about what happened that night.

"Look, I'm tired. Can you please leave me alone?" I say.

She immediately rises to her feet. She slams the chair in an attempt to appear angry but instead comes across as... sweet.

"Look, Infinity, I didn't mean to..." I try to explain.

"Some of us are fighting hard to live, Luke, while you are fighting hard to die."

I feel a great pain runs through my spine.

"Have a nice day." She slams the door.

5 Days After He Shot Himself

"Three-Eyed Monster"

Loneliness
burns your guts up
like a vicious disease.

You shouldn't have left
and I shouldn't have loved you.

Regret can
cripple you.
Remorse can
debilitate you.

Lately, I have been
wondering
about the wrong turns
I took
that led me to
this loneliness
and sadness.

I have been wondering
how ugly I am.
And how I am
incapable
of being loved.

I feel so ugly
too often
I touch my face
to look for
my third
eye.

5 Days After He Shot Himself

"Same Old Pain"

Everything is different
but nothing has changed.

The same old pain lingers
as the loneliness smiles at my wounds.

These days I have been recalling
long drives
and your favorite music playing.
You were inhaling smoke, and
I was inhaling you.
Memories carry more weight
than bones.
I can barely walk now,
but I walk.
The world is full of madness,
but I live.

Every time I talk about you
to anyone
I taste bitterness in my tongue.

Answer me,
What have you done to me?
And how can you
live with yourself?

6 Days After He Shot Himself

"The Suicidal"

I was suicidal,
and people didn't
even know.

I left the stove on while took my afternoon nap.
I loved you.
I started driving without putting my seatbelt on.
I loved you.
I stood at the edge of every cliff I reached.
I loved you.

I did all types of
self-harm
and the most dangerous thing
I have ever done
to hurt myself
was loving you.

7 Days After He Shot Himself

"The Sunset"

"Could you guys work on updating the vending machine items?" Outside my room, I hear Infinity's voice. She's getting another snack from the vending machine. She eats far too much for her thin frame.

"Infinity, you just finished your chemo. Don't eat that right now; you'll throw up." I hear Sandy say.

I get up. Thinking, it's not a bad idea to eat a snack now. Or do I want to see Infinity? I get out of my room and watch Infinity looking at the chocolate bar disposing of the vending machine, she looks as innocent as a little kid.

"It's my turn," I say.

She takes a step back without saying a word. She's busy unwrapping her chocolate bar. She looks paler today. Sicker.

"You appear to be in better shape today, Mr. Adams," Sandy says. I feel a pinch in my stomach.

"Thank you," I say as I insert cash into the vending machine. I'm not sure if I want to eat anything. I have no idea what I'm doing.

WHAT ARE YOU TRYING TO DO? DO YOU WANT TO GET HURT?

"You finally decided to join the living and eat?" Infinity asks cynically.

"I suppose." I'm hesitant to respond.

"I'm not going to eat it, you know?" She stares at the chocolate bar in her hand. "I'm just going to pretend that I'm eating it."

I don't ask why.

I know why.

"After chemo, my stomach feels strange. I'm a huge foodie. Even pretending to eat it makes me happy. The most difficult part of chemotherapy is the loss of appetite.

If I survive this cancer, I plan to spend the rest of my life eating.”

I feel bad. I really do.

“Tell me Blue Eyes, Do you want to feel alive?” She asks with a serious look expecting a genuine response from me.

I feel intimidated. “I’m not sure,” I answer.

“No,” she takes the candy bar I just got from the vending machine off my hand. “I need a real answer. Do you want to feel alive?”

“That’s the best I can come up with, Infinity. I’m honestly not sure.”

She cracks a melancholy smile. She has an enticing smile with white teeth that contrast with her yellowish light skin. She glances at her watch and adds, “It’s time. Come along with me.” She takes my hand in hers and begins walking quickly. I follow.

Sandy yells, “Infinity Rosefield, Slow down, you just finished your chemo.”

We enter the elevator, still holding my hand as if I were a lost child. She presses the eleventh floor, the hospital’s top floor.

Moments of awkward silence in the elevator made her realize that she’s still holding my hand. She let go. And I wish she didn’t.

The elevator opens. “Follow me.” She says.

She makes her way to the emergency exit.

“I don’t think we are allowed to go there,” I say.

“We are not allowed to go there, but we are sick.” She giggles. “If we get caught, no one will punish us. I’m just going to pretend that I am getting sicker.” She says, smiling again. And there is a part of me that enjoys this thrill.

She slowly unlocks the emergency door and begins ascending the stairs. She seems exhausted, but she does not stop trying to hide her fatigue.

I’m still following her.

We finally reach another door which I believe leads

to the roof.

I can see the sunset tint reflected on her white skin as she opens the door. She raises her arms, as if the sun is hugging her, and moves slowly towards the edge of the roof, which overlooks the city's stunning skyline.

I feel like a lost child who has no idea what to do.

"This is the closest I've ever come to feeling alive." Finally, she breaks her quiet.

I take a glance at her. Then there's the vista. She looks so free and beautiful.

"Tell me, Luke, how many sunsets have you seen?" She asks.

I think about it and I realize that I haven't seen a sunset in a very long time. I hated sunsets. I hated the world. I hated to live. I've always walked with my head down.

"I don't know," I answer. "Not many, I guess."

She is still opening her arms. I look at her, and I notice that she starts to cry quietly.

"I'm scared that this will be my last sunset." She cries out in pain.

Depression

Any two lost souls that find each other after a long life of sorrow and pain generate boundless power. That power could cure diseases and perform miracles, but it could also melt mountains and burn bridges. It has the potential to turn you into an addict and destroy you. It's like playing with fire for the sake of being warm when you already know that the fire will burn you to ashes. Can you feel how he is shivering remembering his frigid days? Can you feel his loneliness? Can you hear the echoes in his empty hospital room? Can you feel his longing to talk to someone every night and tell them that he couldn't even end his own life?

Luke understands that he will never be happy. He might not be dead, but he is lost. And sometimes the two are interchangeable. He understands that his wounds will not heal. He knows far too much to stay alive. He knows far too much to be found again. And when you're lost or dead, you cling to the rope that will bring you out of the darkness and into the light. You'll need any warmth that will keep you from shivering.

Infinity is that rope for Luke.
And his light.
And also, she is his fire.

And fire will either burn you,
or die trying.

8 Days After He Shot Himself

"Rejection"

There is an attachment
to this disease
I carry in my skull
I hold it every night
and dance with it
like
broken lovers.

This world has rejected me
but my demons
could never
reject me.
They cuddle me
in the middle of the night
and keep me warm
with
anxiety and worry.

I'm not empty;
I'm full of
beautiful
catastrophes
and death
and some other
beautiful things
too.

9 Days After He Shot Himself

"Dealing with the Past"

I found myself telling Infinity things I hadn't even told Dr. Richard. Maybe it's her eyes, the way they sparkle with care and hope every time I tell her about something from my past. Perhaps because she has cancer, and I know my secrets will die with her.

It's nearly midnight. The hospital lights are turned off, and she is in my room. We'd been chatting for hours, but it felt like only minutes. I found myself telling her everything there was to know about Harmony, my family, the incident, and the day I shot myself.

"The issue is, I don't think I'll ever be able to forget my past," I admit to Infinity, feeling wonderfully exposed. "And I can't live with it since the future isn't going to be that different. It's only one line; the line of my life. The future is simply stretched from the past. And I wanted to cut this line. I want to end it."

"I'm not saying you should ignore your past. I'm asking you to let go," she says.

"I'm not sure what the difference is."

"You hear a lot of people telling you to let go most of the time. You hear the words 'move on' and 'get over it'. When we are told to let go, we link it with forgetting it ever happened. That is precisely why it becomes so difficult. Moving on isn't about running away from the past; it's about accepting it. Your memories are as real as your flesh is to you. Memories cannot be erased. However, you have to learn to live with them. Letting go means learning to live in the face of adversity. Acceptance comes from letting go. What happened to you happened, but how can you go on? The more you acknowledge what happened to you, the easier it is to accept it. So, instead of picturing your life without anxiety, you have to acknowledge it. Accept it. Love it. Live with it. Your anxiety is part of who you are. Find a way to live with it. That's what I'm doing with my cancer."

She casually mentions her cancer. She had come to terms with her sickness a long time ago. And she is still fighting it fiercely.

"It's quite difficult, Infinity. My anxiety and Depression do not appear on my body in the same way that cancer does. They're ripping me apart from the inside out. Most of the time, I don't think my pain is worth feeling."

"Just because people don't see your pain, doesn't mean you aren't allowed to feel it. It is your pain, not theirs. Who are they to pass judgment on what your heart truly feels? You owe it to yourself to feel what your heart needs to feel to heal itself."

My entire body shivers because she feels so familiar. Reality collides with dreams. Sometimes I wonder if she is a real person. Or maybe I'm dead, and this is heaven, and she's an angel.

12 Days After He Shot Himself

"Abandon Places"

And we wander,
running and walking
and crawling sometimes,
searching for love
in abandoned places
where anything
can be found
but love.
We wander
with the hope of
one day
we will receive
the love that
we once gave.

15 Days After He Shot Himself

"My Pills"

I want to know more about you.

I want to breathe you in
and out.

I want to smoke you
and take you
like
pills
before lunch,
and after dinner.

I want to know
how you fill your lungs
with so much
love
and breathe it all into me.

I want you to
call my name
so your voice makes me
forget all about my
buried childhood pain.

Let's meet again
and talk about our feeling
and all our lost lovers
and the love we found
and life
and death
and all the other
beautiful things.

16 Days After He Shot Himself

"Anew"

So this is how it feels like
to love someone new
with an old heart that
is barely beating
and already broken.

The closer I get to you,
the more I can't breathe.
So I beg you
to stay close to me
tonight
and every other night
even if you watch me
breathless
I beg you
to stay and
breathe love
to this old heart.

Love me
anew.

18 Days After He Shot Himself

"Clowns and Devils"

Life is insignificant. Nothing happens for a reason. Things just happen because they want to happen. Good or bad. We are not connected. Nothing matters. Our souls are full of filth. There is a constant fight between the living and the dying. The living eagerly wants a taste of death and the dying desperately wants to stay alive. It's a circus that nobody watches. Clowns and devils. Everybody searches for love but never finds it. Love exists only in books and in the mind of the mad ones. Like hamsters on wheels, we keep running after people that don't want us only to get burned by the same fire over and over again. Then we cry out in agony, wishing death on ourselves because we believe we don't deserve to be alive. You stop asking to be happy and you start praying to feel less so you can live through a tough day and face this ugly world.

I'm not pessimistic; I just notice things that others don't. I have seen death and even worse things. Nothing is worse than being alive with unbearable pain that consumes you at all hours of the day and night and knowing no one is aware of it. Depression is so insidious because it tricks you into seeing things that aren't real until you reach the point where you don't know what's real anymore.

I'm not sure I want to be alive. But, to be honest, I don't want to die either. I'd like to be saved. I want to heal the suffering inside of me. I'm not sure why the mountains aren't moving to save me. Am I not worth saving?

20 Days After He Shot Himself

"Terminal"

"The most difficult aspect of having stage four cancer is that no one ever acknowledges the elephant in the room, which is that my cancer is terminal. All of these chemo sessions are just slowing things down to give me a few extra days." Infinity expresses herself for the first time in full about her cancer.

She sounds desperate for the first time since I met her. Her beautiful smile has vanished. Perhaps my Depression is contagious.

We're back on the hospital's rooftop. This is now our usual spot. We're holding hands. I'm not sure how we got to this point. The only thing I know is that she needs me as much as I need her right now. And it feels so damn good.

I wish I could tell her something that would make her feel better or take her pain away; instead, I hold her hands even tighter. She rests her head on my shoulder.

"Everyone is wondering why I did it," I say; I feel so transparent with her. "The answer is simple. When the pain takes over the mind with a little help from Depression and anxiety, the mind tends to produce thoughts and solutions to get rid of that pain. It's our survival instinct. Take few more pills. Call your ex. Temporary solutions that will ease the pain for a while, but then another wave of pain comes, and the mind begins to suggest a permanent solution that feels right for the state of mind at that time. I did it because I was in a lot of pain."

She lets out a sigh. I do as well. We're in perfect sync.

"Are you still in pain?" She asks.

"Not while I'm with you," I say.

"Maybe you should learn how to live, and I should start learning how to die." She says. "You teach me death, and I will teach you all the other beautiful things."

Depression

Human beings are pitiful. They are waiting for someone to save them because they're too weak to save themselves.

Nobody will come to your rescue. My dear, you are not here to be saved. You've come to suffer. And to be consumed. You are here to feel all the anguish you're meant to feel.

I've always been truthful with you and will continue to do so. I haven't been feeling well recently. I've been feeling quite weak. I'm not fond of this new girl or how she makes me feel or how she makes Luke feel. She makes me feel insignificant. She manages to make Luke forget about me. But I will find my way around, I always do. And they always come and leave. And I'm always there.

You feel sorry for him, Don't you? I don't blame you. I mean after what he has been through, he deserves some happiness. But he deserves me as well. I was with him when no one else was. I was with him when everyone else abandoned him. We wept together many nights. I preyed on him, my Luke. I protected him. What will happen to him if that girl leaves him? No one will be there for him but me, my Luke.

22 Days After He Shot Himself

"New Colors"

She found me broken and withered
and said,
I see you from afar
you are three colors
blue, like the color of your bruises.
Black, like the color under your eyes.
Red, because you have been bleeding for
some time now.
It must be lonely
living only in three colors
covered in darkness.
A faded tragedy,
my dear.

But tonight,
I will love you
until I color you with
new beautiful colors.
Gold will be the color of your blood.
Lilac will be the color of your breath.
Emerald will be the color of your eyes.

I promise
heavens will look at you
and tremble
with envy.

24 Days After He Shot Himself

"The Truth About Love"

Most of us
are consumed
by love,
annihilated.

Few of us
are
lucky enough
to be
loved
back.

25 Days After He Shot Himself

"Madness and Chaos"

"Why are you running away from me?"
"Because I'm scared of you
and all the things
I'm feeling towards you.
I'm terrified of the idea
that I could never unlove you.
The way you
silenced all my demons,
I'm not used to
living a life so quiet
and beautiful.
I'm used to madness and
chaos.
You are what life is,
and I'm used to death."

27 Days After He Shot Himself

"One More Week"

Meeting a new individual is like arriving on an unknown island just waiting to be discovered. Every day is a new adventure, a fresh opportunity to explore their regions and swim at their shores.

This is how I've been feeling lately with Infinity. We found each other in a hopeless place. We met at the crossroad of death and life.

I go to her room and knock on her door.

"She is not here." The nurse says.

I wonder where she is.

"Are you Luke?" A familiar voice asks. I look behind me. A woman that looks like an older version of Infinity is smiling at me. *Her mother.*

"Yes, I am," I respond confidently, feeling a little happy that Infinity mentioned me to her.

She looks around as if she's terrified someone would notice us together. "Come on, let's go inside." She explains.

I follow her as she opens the door to Infinity's room.

She takes a seat in front of Infinity's bed. The bed is unmade, and there is uneaten breakfast on the table. Something isn't quite right.

"Is everything okay, Mrs. Rosefield? Where is Infinity?"

"She is with her father," she says. "He's finishing up her paperwork so he can take her home." Her voice is filled with unsaid pain, and her eyes are tearful as she speaks. "The doctor informed us that all of her treatments had failed to control her cancer." She bursts into tears. "He believes that she has only a few days to live."

My heart is pounding really fast and I feel irregularity in my breathing. Another anxiety attack. HELLO AGAIN. No. No. I can't do this right now. I need to be strong. My tears started falling uncontrollably. I'm not crying, I feel like I'm melting.

She wipes her tears with her sleeve. "We haven't told her yet, Luke. And we have no intention of doing so." She spoke in a stern tone. "We informed her that her cancer is currently in remission. We are going to make her last days as comfortable as possible." She sobs even more.

"How many days are there left?" I say this, choking on the words. I'm still trying to swallow my tears.

"The doctor told us she will not live more than a week..." She is struggling to find the right words to say. But there are no right words. "She loves you, Luke. She only talks about you. Please make sure you love her back in the coming days."

"I love her too, Mrs. Rosefield." That all I can say to her.

The door opens. And there she is. Infinity, looking beautiful as ever.

"Yay, you are here." She says. She seems to be in better shape today. Her cheeks had become a deeper shade of pink. Her eyes have become more glistening. This is the effect of hope on people.

I can't believe this is happening.

"Are you ready to spend our last day on the hospital's rooftop?" She teases.

I feel like I'm bleeding. I'm dizzy and nauseated.

This is it, the end of everything.

Depression

Human beings tend to forget who they are when they're happy. Time becomes irrelevant. They disconnect from their inner selves and connect to the one moment that makes them happy. Until this moment is over and they remember who they are. Weak. Powerless. Small.

Luke had forgotten he was in the hospital. He acted as if he was living in heaven. He was getting better but not because he was working on getting better. He forgot his sickness, his reality, because of her. He got attached to her and the things he feels whenever she's around. Like a drug addict, he always goes back for more.

But what if there are no more drugs? What will Luke do? I'm too familiar with him. He will not survive her. He will remember his sickness again. He will get down on his knees and pray that his pain would stop. He will feel all this emptiness that was being filled by whatever she was giving him. He will hear nothing but her echoes. He will not eat again. He will not sleep again.

Luke's death will be disclosed at the same time as Infinity's. They will be perfectly in harmony, even after death.

Why wouldn't I help him?

Luke can't be saved.

He chose her and he has to live with the consequences.

28 Days After He Shot Himself

"My Anxiety Told Me So"

I sing my favorite song and dance in the middle of the store. I can feel that people are staring at me because my anxiety told me so. My Depression wants me to go back to my bed. I'm frail because the other side of the bed is always empty. But I'm strong because I can still sing.

I'm the embodiment of a walking disaster; I bend and break but then fight back, clawing my way out of bed every night, trying to get away from the monsters under my bed. Inside my head, my two closest friends, anxiety and Depression, sleeping with me. Oh, how I feel loved and hated at the same time. It's always a never-ending battle, a war with no deaths but mine. I want to get out and fight but my anxiety holds me as a hostage inside my insecurities, and my Depression is pointing the gun at my head. My shivering fingers are laid upon the trigger. Shall I pull the trigger? I don't know because my Depression wants me to die. But my anxiety reminds me that I'm afraid of death.

What a beautiful battle. My insomnia and my body are at odds. I fall asleep without warning, yet I can only sleep for a minute until my anxiety wakes me up and my Depression keeps me awake. I want to take control of the gun pointing at me. I don't want to die but sometimes I want to, because death is merciful when you are not doing much of being alive.

Am I really alive?

30 Days After He Shot Himself

"One Last Time"

We lie down under the warmth of the orange sunset hue on the hospital's rooftop one last time. We are happy and healthy. Our illness has sunk into the depths of the ocean. We've never felt more alive.

"What are you planning to do after we leave?" She asks.

"I'm planning to be with you," I respond. And I really mean it.

She cracks a smile. A warm smile; she looks exhausted, yet because the sun is reflected on her gorgeous pale skin, she looks like an angel.

"Let me rephrase," she adds. "What are we going to do when we leave here?"

"We can go on a trip," I say. All I want is to be closer to her during her final days.

"My parents won't allow me to travel because I'm too sick."

"I can talk to them. We don't have to travel. We can take a short trip to an island nearby just for few days."

She looks at me. And then the sky.

I keep looking at her.

"I have always wanted to go to Sapphire Island. Although it is only two hours away, I have not had the chance to visit."

"Then we will go to the Sapphire Island."

"My parents..." She reminds me.

"I'll talk to them," I say.

We exchange glances for a few seconds as if we're staring at something we're trying too hard to discover. I'm intrigued by her. And all I can think about is how I want to spend the rest of my life with her.

The rest of her life.

31 Days After He Shot Himself

"Time"

Time crushes me
every night again.

I'm scared and awed at
its quickening pace
with every passing day.

Suddenly, all my words were
of love,
and all my love was
for you.

34 Days After He Shot Himself

"Life and Death"

"The only thing I want to do now that I'm out of the hospital is to take Infinity to Sapphire Island," I tell Dr. Richard. This is the hospital's final session. I'll be leaving tonight.

"Do you love her?" He asks.

I stutter. "Yes. I do love her." I say. "And I know what you're going to say, it's practically impossible to love someone in a month, but Infinity and I don't have enough time."

"Love, Luke, can never be measured by time. Some people try to feel something for each other for their entire lives, while others feel everything in a matter of days. When it comes to love, time is irrelevant."

"I'm getting better with her, Dr. Richard. She is healing me."

"I'm worried about the aftermath of it all. What will happen to you when it all comes to an end?"

"I'm not ready to discuss it yet." I strive hard to keep these ideas at bay. I refuse to think that Infinity is dying.

"Luke, death is part of life. You, of all people, should be aware of it by now. Love her. Go on this trip with her. However, you must accept life as much as you accept death. The two are intertwined. The starting and finishing lines."

"It's easier for me to accept my death. It is hard to accept it when it comes to the closest people in my life." I say as my spine shivers by the thought of her death. "They go, and I am left with all the pain."

"However, pain is temporary, and so is life. That is something you must accept. You must survive. You must fight. Go to this trip, Luke. Learn how to live. And how to say goodbye and deal with the pain."

35 Days After He Shot Himself

"Car Crash"

What I ache for
every night
is your arms
cradled around me
like a car crash.

She is so beautiful
I swear

and I know
beautiful things
don't last.

35 Days After He Shot Himself

"Questions and Answers"

Does she know that
she makes my life
higher
like I'm living
in the sky?

Does she know
that I ache
for the way
she laughs
and the way her voice
takes home
in my ears?

Does she know
that I craved death
before I met her
but now
there's nothing I want
more than
being alive?

40 Days After He Shot Himself

"All the Other Beautiful Things"

I've been to Sapphire Island more times than I can remember; it's the gateway for our town's lovers and loners, but this time I feel as if it's my first visit.

It's her. Infinity. She makes me notice the small beautiful things that I used to overlook. I feel as if I was blind and have only recently begun to see again.

"Look at the sky, Luke." She says. "It's a beautiful shade of blue, like your eyes."

Yes, it is.

"Can we ride a horse?" She asks.

You certainly can.

"I'm craving ice cream. I'll have pistachio and you'll have double chocolate." She demands.

She is brimming with life. I almost forgot that she's dying. She believes her cancer is under control, but she is constantly battling the pain. She's clinging to life. And It seems impossible that she will ever let go.

And I can't help but wonder; I was trying to kill myself while many others are trying to stay alive. All of the things I didn't want to see. This beautiful life and all the other beautiful things. They are there. All I need to do is see them.

Will I be able to see all of this beauty
when she's gone?

41 Days After He Shot Himself

"Suicidal Love"

Some say
that my love for you was
suicidal
in all the beautiful
ways possible.

I remember the day
we were riding a jetski
in the middle of the raging sea
and a storm came
death was near
you wear holding me tight
and we were about to be swallowed.
I wasn't scared of death
because the idea of dying with you
was so poetic.

And the other time
We were on a cable car
22,322 feet
above the ground
I was beyond happy
because we were together
and you were scared
"If we fall we will die," you said.
I smiled.
And the truth is,
I wasn't scared
because
if we fall,
we would still
die together.

43 Days After He Shot Himself

"After Death"

"What do you believe will happen after death?" Infinity asks.

We're lying down on the beach, watching the sunset. We decided to return to town tomorrow because she isn't feeling well today. *Is this her last sunset?*

"Emptiness. Nothingness. Darkness. A complete absence. A relief." I answer her. And I understand I'm terrifying her the instant these words leave my mouth.

She rests her head on my shoulder. A surge of warmth overcomes my body.

"I'm ready to die, Luke." Her words pierce me. The warmth has given way to frigid spikes. I'm in pain.

"Don't say this," I say, kissing her forehead. "You love life and life loves you back. You showed me how beautiful this life is. It truly is. I see everything in new vibrant colors. I'm loving life because of you, Infinity."

"And I've learned from you that death is beautiful too," she says. "Death is merciful."

"Don't give up on me now," I say, holding her cold, anguished face. I cry, like a child pleading for help.

She places her icy fingers on my cheeks and whispers, "Luke, you are going to live a very wonderful life," she says while crying herself. "And you're going to meet a fortunate girl who will make you the happiest guy ever."

"I don't want anyone else, Infinity; I want you."

"I will miss you," she says as she wipes my tears away with the delicate tip of her thumb.

"Please, Infinity, don't leave me here alone."

"I'm in a lot of pain, Luke. My skin feels like it's being pulled off. This cancer is eating my bones, and I'm carrying all of this anguish on my own. Everything hurts me today, and I knew the moment I walked out of the hospital that I was dying with no hope. But you, Luke, you are my hope."

You are my hope too.

"Promise me, Luke. Promise me you'll live after I'm gone. Promise me."

I hesitate.

Do I really want to live after she's gone?

"Please, Luke. I would be smiling down to you from heaven if I see you trying to live a long life. Promise me."

"I promise," I say

not sure if I mean it.

44 Days After He Shot Himself

"A Celebration"

Do I still love you?
Do I want to die?
Different questions,
same answers.

Lately, I have been thinking a lot
about you.
How warm was the bed,
when I laid next to you,
and how cold my grave is.
How your life was
a celebration
and mine was
a funeral.
How you colored me in,
and I filled your days
with darkness.

Life is anything but fair.
One seeks life and finds death,
while others seek death and find life.

45 Days After He Shot Himself

"Fists and Wounds"

I used to think love
was my fists through
a wall,
until you took my hands,
kissed them,
and healed
every open wound I had.

I will never forget that part of you,
The part that cared
about everyone else.
And I will never forget
all the other parts too.
You are simply unforgettable.

You were the first one who made me feel
as if I belong to something
more than the chaos of life.

When you hugged me the first time,
every wound in me
was stitched back together.

Thank you for that and everything else.
Every scar of my body felt like it was
part of something greater
life started to have a meaning,
and death too.

46 Days After He Shot Himself

"Overdosing"

You called me sugar
and I dissolved
in your grace.

We pretended
we were
alive
until we suddenly
were
at dawn
overdosing on love
and all the other
beautiful things
your love
offered.

47 Days After He Shot Himself

"The Finale"

4:11 PM

Infinity said very little on the trip back from the island. She is shivering and groaning in pain. And I wish I could take all of her pain with me to the grave. I hope that she lives a long, happy life. I wish I could take her death. I feel helpless.

She hasn't smiled since we boarded. It's as though death is savagely devouring pieces of her. I can feel her life slowly leaving her body. I'm shivering along with her. My life and her death are in sync together. It's happening. My lungs are closing. Hello, anxiety. HELLO. Please this isn't the right time. SHE IS GOING TO DIE, LUKE. YOU WILL BE LEFT ALONE WITH ALL THE PAIN THAT SHE WILL LEAVE FOR YOU. WHAT HAVE YOU DONE?

"Hold on, Infinity, we're nearly there," I say as I brush my fingers over her hair. She's as cold as ice.

"I could... stay... in your arms... forever." She says, and my heart aches.

Death is cruel.

7:27 PM

Her parents are at the pier, waiting for us. I'm carrying Infinity to their car; she's surprisingly light for her size. She is no longer speaking, only shivering from the pain.

"Oh, my baby. My sweet baby," her mother cries.

Her father is fixing the backseat for her. I lay her down.

"I've missed you." She tells her parents, unawakened.

"I will ride with you," I tell her father. He nods

8:03 PM

This time, it is her father who is carrying her. Mrs. Rosefield is still sobbing. Infinity is half dead, half alive.

And I think I'm half alive, half dead.

"Please come inside, my dear." Her mother welcomes me in.

"I will give you some space," I say. "I will be around. if anything happens, please call me."

Her mother nods and shuts the door.

As I walk down the steps of Infinity's front door, I realize our journey has come to an end. I have nothing new but the memories that will haunt me for the rest of my life. WHAT HAVE YOU DONE LUKE? YOU SHOULDN'T HAVE GONE ON THIS TRIP. THOSE MEMORIES WILL BE YOUR DEATH. I might not see Infinity ever again. YOU WILL NEVER SEE HER AGAIN. She might die tonight. SHE WILL. WHAT WOULD YOU DO? I won't feel her skin and I won't hear her laugh. I slump, scarcely breathing, at her door.

YOU CAN'T BREATHE. YOU ARE HAVING A HEART ATTACK.

I Inhale. I exhale.

I cry as I lean against the door. I feel like I've lost a large part of myself that I've spent my entire life trying to find.

I weep
until the pain overtakes my body
and I fall asleep.

47 Days After He Shot Himself

"Hung"

I love you
as much as
death
love the sick
and money loves the rich,
and hunger loves the poor.
I love you
as much
as we
are hung
to a life
that will leave us
under the ground
at the end.

Depression

Happiness is a delusion. Everyone is running trying to find happiness until they come back to me, weeping. And I will be there to comfort them. I will always be there.

The stench of death is here. He can almost taste it. Do you smell it? No? Don't worry, not everyone can.

I knew Luke would eventually come back to me. And he would fall again into my void. This time even harder.

You cannot escape the darkness. You can't escape Depression. The curse will make everyone around you suffer, starting with you. You have blood on your hands. You shouldn't have left me. You shouldn't have escaped.

It's funny, for him to think that he can run away from his past and his sadness. A man can never escape his mind and reality. He wanders, trying to find meaning for his desperate life, and he comes back again, into my arms.

Come, child. Take my hand.
Welcome home, Luke.
You have been missed.

47 Days After He Shot Himself

"The Finale"

5:03 AM

WAKE UP. YOU ARE ALL ALONE. SHE IS GONE.
SHE IS GONE.
LUKE.
"Luke," Infinity's father says quietly, attempting to wake me up. I'm still outside their front door.
Did I sleep here?
"Come inside, son." He says. His eyes are red. He was crying.
Oh, my God. Infinity.
I don't ask because I'm scared of the answer.
I follow him inside the house. Their whole house smells like Infinity.
I can hear her mother sobbing.
And I immediately realize that Infinity is gone.
I follow the voice. Her mother is sitting on the couch, wailing. Her hands are covering her face as if she is trying to escape reality.
My legs are giving up. I take a seat.
"Thank you very much, Luke." Her mother says, tearfully. "Thank you for giving her such a beautiful end."
I've run out of words. I can't believe Infinity is gone.
What about me? How will I go on?
"She left letters for all of us," Mr. Rosefiled says, standing next to me, I almost didn't notice him. "I believe she wrote them in the middle of the night before..." He stutters. He can't say the words.
Everything feels like a nightmare.
He hands my letter to me.
I take it and leave.
I need to be alone.

Dear Luke,

If you get this letter, it means that I'm gone.

I know you're sad, and you're going to torture yourself over the news of my death, but please don't. My death is a mercy because I couldn't take any more pain. I was waiting for it, but I wasn't prepared for it. It's the end of a long war with many battles lost. I fought bravely, and now I've accepted defeat and surrendered. It's simply time for me to go. And one day it will be your time to go as well, but first, you must fight your battles. And I don't mean just surviving; I mean truly living. Luke Adams, you must live, with or without me.

Begin your life with forgiving. It's time to let go of the past by forgiving those who have harmed you severely that you can't go on with all your wounds. Forgive them and move forward. Your wounds will begin to heal, and you will be able to rise again, alive, ready to be hurt again because you know you will survive no matter what.

Someone will come along and make you forget all that happened in the past, but only if you let go of the idea of being with someone.

Thank you for giving me the best last days on earth.

I'm looking down at you right now.

Live your life for both of us.

Yours

Infinity.

48 Days After He Shot Himself

"The Broken"

I have been there before
with the same broken bones
and heart.
I'm dancing with tears in my eyes,
and different tears in
my skin.
Does this how it feels to be alive?

We aren't meant to be broken.
We aren't meant to be broken.

48 Days After He Shot Himself

"A Beautiful Poem"

I wrote a beautiful poem
but then I lit a cigarette and
burned it.
The poem was about you
and how beautiful you always looked
how you loved life more than you loved me
and I was okay with that
for I loved life because I loved you.

I burned that beautiful poem
to ashes
because I can't stand beautiful things anymore.

Beautiful things always
tend to break my heart.

50 Days After He Shot Himself

"Laughter"

There is a tomb
in my ear
that holds your laughter.
I'll never forget
the melody of your voice
and how you used to
wake the birds up every morning
and make them sing.

Whether you're here
or in heaven,
or even in hell,
I wish you would know
that your laughter
still helps me smile.

51 Days After He Shot Himself

"Perfume"

I found you
and lost you
in a breeze.
Life isn't fair
and death isn't too.

I'm wearing
death like a perfume now
because it carries your smell.

Wherever you are
I hope you carry the
same smile
that kept me
in awe
every night.

Wherever you are,
I hope
death
will eventually
carry me to you.

52 Days After He Shot Himself

"Doorstep"

It takes few tries
of falling in love
to realize
that love isn't a game.

Love is a matter
of death
and life.

Either love is going to save you
or it is going bring death
to your doorstep.

And sometimes
it's really hard
to tell the difference.

Too often
looking for love
is a form
of self-harm.

72 Days After He Shot Himself

"Loneliness"

Loneliness is beautiful
but sometimes
it chokes you,
breaks your bones
and twists
your spine.
you start screaming
from the pain
until it makes you
think of
ending your own pathetic life
and if you do it
you start to wonder whether
anyone will
care
or even
notice.

NIRVANA

In a world filled with sickness, anger, envy, and death, I created my own Nirvana. I'm out of the loop of sorrow. I'm alive now. I'm breathing in and out where my past is encased in a little dark circle that I won't dare to enter. It is there, and I am aware of it, but it can no longer harm me. I'm somewhere between death and life and I feel more alive than I have ever been in a long time.

Present Day

"Unwritten Poem"

I write you,
then unwrite you
on paper
and to the winds.

I have so much
ungiven love
for you,
and to you.

I gave up on
all my writings
and books.
I have never
stopped loving you.
I still find you
in the small space
between the clock's hands
4:05 AM
the time of death,
the time you left.

I will never stop
writing about you.

I have written so little
and I will write more
to you, and for you.

Present Day

"The Winds"

I tell the winds
how much I miss you
and they don't answer me.
I don't think they believe
a love like this could exist.
But it does exist
between the earliest hour in the morning
and the latest hour in the night
you visit me
and I can smell you,
almost.
And I can remember the way your lips tasted,
almost.
This life has torn me apart
and oh, how much easier it could have been
if we spent it together.
But the winds have taken you away
so I tell them
how much
I miss you
in hope
that they will
bring you back to me.

Present Day

"I'm Good"

She dared to ask me
      "How are you doing?"
      "I'm healing, from you.
      deliberately."
I answered.

Look, I'm here to tell you that I'm good. I'm doing better than I was the day before. And I'm confident that I'll get better with time because I believe in myself. And here's something you may not know: I've been to hell and back seven times. And I've been through tougher waves than this one. This is mild. And I'm a fighter. Just because I cried that doesn't mean I'm weak. Just because I broke that doesn't mean I won't be fixed. I'll put myself back together piece by piece and fix myself. No, I don't want you or anybody else to fix me this time. I'll handle the damage you've done to me on my own because I know I'm strong. And your pain is a mosquito bite compared to what I have been through before meeting you. And neither you nor hundreds of other selfish people will be able to change me. I was good to you. And I will be good to someone else. I will stay good and do good because I believe one good act of kindness can change the world. If your self-centered outlook on life can't accept that fact, then go to hell. I'm not here to please you or anyone else. I'm simply here to make the world a better place, one act of kindness at a time.

Present Day

"The End of Ryan Adams"

"Hello, brother."

"What do you want, Luke? Both of our parents are dead. Nothing connects us anymore." He looks at me with icy, dead eyes.

"You are mistaken. We share the same blood. You will always be my brother..."

"I don't want to be your brother."

"I don't want that either," I say, and I can tell by the look on his face that he didn't see that coming. "Look, Ryan, this is the last time you'll see me," I add. "I just want to say a few things I should have said a long time ago."

He glances at me, perplexed and terrified of what I'm about to say.

"You're not half as good as you think you are. And that it is your sickness..." I tell him. And I feel relieved.

"If you don't stop talking right now, I'll shatter your face."

"You no longer frighten me, Ryan, and I'm not done talking," I scream. "You never listened to me. You've never been by my side when I was at my lowest. I needed you. But you always thought that you are better than me, thanks to Father. And the truth is that you are nothing more than a college dropout who thought he had a football talent but failed as well."

"Watch your mouth, little brother."

"And what will you do to me if I don't? Beat me up to death as you did to your ex-wife? You are a monster. I saw her hospital reports. She had broken ribs and fractured bones. I can't believe that my own blood is capable of hurting someone like that. I can't believe you are my brother."

"Leave now, or I swear.."

"Our mother was in desperate need of your love and support while she was on her death bed but you refused to see her. She was crying and calling your name the night she died. And that's where I knew that you are truly a monster."

"Guard, return me to my cell. Take me out of here. I'm done with this boy."

"No, Ryan, I'm the one who's finished with you. You are dead to me."

Present Day

"The End of Harmony Deadwood"

"What are you doing here?" Harmony asks as I approach her doorstep. Her lips tremble with anxiety.

"I'm here to talk," I explain.

I'm here to ruin you.

"Sammy is inside; I can't let you in. You are welcome to talk here." She shuts the door, gets a cigarette from her pocket, and lights it.

"I haven't told you this before, Harmony, but you are the most manipulative person I've ever met."

I caught her off guard.

She inhales a thick puff from her cigarette.

"I have tolerated your poison because I was in love with you and please understand that I WAS in love with you, but not anymore. I know what love is now, and it's nothing like the hollow, sick love you pretended giving me. You are a parasite, you move from one man to another so that you can feel good about yourself at the end of the night. You just want to feel that you are wanted and loved while you know deep inside that you can't be loved enough, because you hate yourself."

She puts out the cigarette and tries to open the door, but I grab her arm before she can reach for it.

"I'm not done talking," I say.

"Let go of my arm, or I'll scream." She says.

"You won't scream," I say. "Because you don't want Sammy to know how sick you are."

"What do you want from me?" She sobs.

"I want you to understand how sick you are. I'd like you to go to counseling before you hurt someone else the way you hurt me. I'd like you to quit treating guys like puppets. I want you to learn that people, unlike you, have feelings, and your manipulative ways of loving them will end up hurting them."

I let go of her arm.

"Don't play with someone's heart if you have no intentions for loving them with all your heart."

She runs back inside.

I leave.

And this time, I truly leave, with no shred of Harmony in me. I let go of her and her poisonous memories.

She shall not haunt me again.

Present Day

"The End of Shawn Morgan"

I knock on the door. Once. Twice.

I feel as if I'm perched on the precipice of a cliff. And I'm about to take the leap. He lives in a beautiful, big house, with a gazebo and a garden. The perfect house. You'd never guess there's a sicko living inside.

A woman opens the door, his wife I assume.

"Are you Mrs. Morgan?" I ask, politely.

"Yes, and who's this?" She delicately answers.

"Can I please speak with Shawn?"

Yes, I did look him up too. When he dropped me off at the hospital the night he visited me, he left his contact information. He most likely thought I'd never ask for him, but I did.

"Are you his friend?" She asks, narrowing her eyes. She probably noticed the age difference.

"He is a friend of someone I know. Is he here? It won't take too long."

"Yes, he is." She smiles. And I think she knows that I'm lying. "I'm going to call him for you. Can you tell me your name?"

"Luke."

She goes inside without closing the door. I walk in uninvited. His house is warm and smells nice. One of his kids is playing video games. He is almost my age when I was raped.

When his father raped me.

Shawn rushes down the stairs.

"I didn't let him in, I'm sorry." I overhear his wife speaking to him in hushed tones.

"Hello, Shawn," I greet him casually. I'm frightening him the same way he once frightened me. I'm the monster who came to knock on your door today.

"Let's talk outside, Luke." I can sense a dreadful panic welling up within him.

"There is nothing to talk about. I'm just dropping by to check how you're doing. How you carried on with your life as if nothing had happened. How you pretend to be normal every day."

"What is he talking about?" His wife asks him. She is terrified.

"How many children have you harmed?" I'm yelling now.

"Luke, please, I beg you," he cries. "Don't do this in front of them."

"And I begged you to stop. I was begging you. You didn't care." My head is filled with rage.

His wife is taken aback. And I notice that his child has paused his video game and is now watching as well.

Shawn begins to cry.

"Just tell me how many children you've harmed."

"Please, Luke." He begs.

"Answer me." I push him. He's crying like a baby. He's afraid of me. I've never felt so powerful. It feels so good.

"It was only you," he says. "And a few others."

My heart is hammering in my chest

"That's it, I promise. I couldn't control myself before, but now I do. I haven't touched a child in a long time. I'm happily married now. I won't let you ruin my family. Leave my house."

"You no longer tell me what to do. You no longer have power over me."

We can both hear the sirens now.

He is in shock.

"The cops are here," I say.

"Please, please, please don't do this."

"I hope you rot in jail; goodbye."

As the cops arrive, I leave his house. I sit in the car, watching as he is being handcuffed and dragged to the rear of the police car.

I feel healed.

Present Day

"Yet"

One day I hit rock bottom
and some other day I discover
that there are memories
I have yet to make,
dreams I have yet to build,
so many days I have yet to live,
and poems I have yet to write.

It takes
one hit
to realize
that.

Present Day

"Plants"

Just like plants
need
sun, air, and water
to grow stronger,
we too,
need resources
beyond ourselves
to be bolder.

Love and kindness.
Support and help.
Forgiveness and understanding.
These are the elements needed
to help us
grow.

One Year Later

"Death and Other Beautiful Things"

There is a way in which this life runs that is beyond our comprehension. We are lines and circles, connected and disconnected. While someone lives a tragedy, someone else is celebrating. While someone is experiencing death, a baby is being born. We are connected and disconnected. And that is one of life's mysteries.

I have saved sixteen people from ending their lives. And I often think, if I had taken my own life, who would have saved them? What if I didn't meet Infinity?
But there's no need to wonder for now. It's all happening. Life has a meaning; we just have to fight a little bit harder.

I have been working in Dr. Richard's office. His idea was to start a suicide prevention group where people who have suicidal thoughts can gather and support one another.
I've been leading this group for about a year and have saved sixteen people. Sixteen people healthy and alive, with families and children. And perhaps the sixteen lives I saved will help save others. We are all connected and disconnected, like life and death.

I enter the room full of people, waiting for me, looking for help. Hello, anxiety, I acknowledge you, but you are no longer in control. Hello depression, my old friend, there is no place for you here anymore. Hello Infinity, this is for you.
"Hello everyone, thank you for putting your trust in me to help you. My name is Luke Adams. And this is my story of how I shot myself. I will tell you all about death and other beautiful things."

It takes a few seconds to save someone's life.
It takes a few seconds to be kind.
It takes a few seconds to reply to a text
and make a phone call.
In a few seconds, you can let the people you love
know that you love them.
Just a few seconds of your time could mean
a lifetime for someone else.
One text from you and they would sleep better.
A few kind words can help them fight stronger.
It takes only a few seconds
to give someone hope again
for a better tomorrow.

It takes a few seconds to save someone's life.

This book saved my life.

Did it save yours?

Did it save you?

DID I SAVE YOU?

The End

Every 40 seconds someone loses their life to suicide.

It's time to make suicide prevention a priority.

1.
Reach out

Encourage them to contact a helpline or someone they could turn to for help, such as a friend, family member, or mentor.

2.
Listen

Pay attention to them and be there for them. Show that you care and that you are there to support them.

3.
Seek Help

Take the guidance of a professional therapist or counselor.

Connect with the author

Website: www.mohamedghazi.com

Email: im@mohamedghazi.com

Instagram: @GhaziTheWriter

Twitter: @M7mdGhazi

Acknowledgment

Nobody believes me when I say this, but I have dreams about what I write. I had a lot of vivid dreams about this book, and the characters felt very real to me. I have dreams about things, and when I wake up, I write about them. This is the way I write.

But what if the dreams stop?

This was one of the most difficult projects I've ever worked on. Because of the pandemic, I couldn't take a vacation for two years. I was unable to travel and suffered from the worst case of writer's block. I couldn't dream any longer. For a few months, I entirely lost my passion for writing, and the prospect of finishing this book seemed insurmountable. We were in the midst of a pandemic, and my life, like everyone else's, was flipped upside down. My anxiety and inability to write had total power over me. And everyone around me was wondering where my book was, but I was embarrassed by my inability to write.

Then I met a few people. And I shattered my own heart. I hate to admit it, but here it is. I broke my own heart in order to feel something. I suddenly found myself in the most toxic group of people. But I started to feel things again. Even if those feelings were pain and discomfort. Then the dreams returned. And that is how this book came to be. And I couldn't have done it without the help of my family. My parents are my rock, and I couldn't be writing this without them. And my dearest friends who have faith in me. And to those poisonous people who broke my heart: without you, I would have no idea how great of a person I am.

I sincerely hope you like this book as much as I did while dreaming about it and creating it. This isn't just a book; it's the thoughts and feelings of the vast majority of people who suffer from anxiety and depression. It's a war, and we must battle on. So, don't give up and keep fighting.

Mohamed Ghazi